Praise for Match-Striking for Beginners

Sometimes life throws you a bone; you meet a person who changes you for the better, who makes the world a better place and makes you believe you can leave a positive impact too. That's Tracey Breeden. In the years I have known her, she has taught me how to not only approach change, but also to evoke it in ways that can make my world as a woman better for all of us. *Match-Striking for Beginners* is one of the most important books I've had the honor of reading. I watched it grow from a flicker of an idea fueled by passion into the honest, thoughtful, raw, yet approachable, work it is now. This roadmap is filled with the truths that motivate us to want better for our world, as well as the ways in which we can do our part to get there. I more than recommend, I insist.

Ginger Scott, **USA Today, Wall Street Journal** *and Amazon bestselling author*

Match-Striking for Beginners is a unique book in the self-improvement space—an inspirational, actionable, and supportive guide to identifying and developing the unique superpower that will propel you forward in life and work. Tracey's career path is not typical, yet the personal stories she uses to demonstrate how she found and used her unique power to make change are entirely relatable. We had the good fortune to work with Tracey in a number of capacities and learned something new every time. Whether you are in the workforce already, or just entering, *Match-Striking for Beginners* is a must read.

Robbie Karp and Jane Randel, Co-Presidents, Karp Randel LLC

I am thrilled to see this book come to life! As someone who: 1) believes in Tracey's vision, 2) needs inspiration to act, and 3) could use a framework for delivering on social change, this book is exactly what I (and so many others) need. The tools, the encouragement, the inspiration garnered from Tracey's lived experiences and other anecdotes, all of it together in one place is going to provide so many people with opportunities to create social change—many who may not otherwise be able to deliver on it.

Jessica Johnson, Director of Product, Match Group

INSPIRED! If you don't walk away feeling like that after reading this book, then you might want to read it again. Tracey's personal anecdotes and vision are clear and social change is what we all need! From start to finish you can't put it down and by the end you are trying to figure out how to help others you may have overlooked in the past. This book is about helping ALL people and I hope it is something that you strive for now too.

LiAnn LaTour, Executive Support Specialist

Getting to know Tracey Breeden in real life is such a joy. But reading Tracey's story and wisdom through these pages is the second-best thing! From personal tales in childhood to making change in professional settings as an adult, Tracey shows us that making an impact is possible if we're willing to speak out. Packed with actionable tips and real-life examples, this book will leave you feeling inspired, empowered, and ready to stand up for what you believe in.

Calen Otto, Author of **The Art of Unruly Travel on a Budget** *and* **Creator of unrulytravel.com**

Tracey's passion and desire to create positive change in the world is always glaringly obvious in any conversation you have with her. In this book, Tracey does a beautiful job of helping you to feel the same desire for change as she does. Tracey doesn't just put statistics in front of you but pairs the painful reality of marginalized groups with actionable tools so that you walk away feeling like you truly can make a difference.

Dianni Hall, Podcast Producer

I had the great fortune of meeting Tracey Breeden through a leadership program that I was facilitating at Uber. The program ended and that was the beginning of a friendship, sisterhood, and commitment to support each other as we lean into our individual and collective work to be a part of much-needed systemic change. Her book illuminates that we have a long way to go to create a harmonious and just world for everyone—no exceptions. And she has bravely offered her life stories in service of shining a light on things we prefer to not see or know about. It also emphasizes what it means to live aligned with values, purpose, and a vision of something better. The best part is that she does not leave us there but rather creates a roadmap and tools for making change happen. And gives us the much-needed hope that it can happen.

Nan Watts, CEO and Founder, Nan Watts Coaching

Tracey, a true catalyst for change and creating safe spaces for all, reveals their transformative journey in this inspiring book, which I hope is just the first of many. As a trailblazing disruptor (have you also listened to their podcast?!), they have revolutionized a range of institutions, from well-established entities like Match.com to cutting-edge startups like Uber—and even their former police department. This book has a unique ability to be both awe-inspiring and accessible. Its collection of powerful stories and life lessons, coupled with a wealth of practical tools, themes, and concepts that breaks down the process of creating change into manageable, step-by-step actions that we can all work to undertake to actively foster safer, more inclusive, and yes, even more fun, communities and organizations. This book rallies a cry for anyone eager to make a significant difference in a world that often overlooks the most vulnerable.

Carley Lake, Co-founder and CEO of Lucky Sweater App and Former Head of Women's Safety Marketing at Uber

The journey of becoming one's own self can be a challenging ride for women. Even having the courage to share our stories—raw, honest, and unfiltered—can be overwhelming, but this is how we truly find authentic connection. In this powerful narrative, Tracey creates a safe space for personal reflection, while providing tools to find our real voice and inspire us to act. As the CEO of a global women's travel community, the book inspires me to stand in a place of hope and ultimately create meaningful and much-needed social change. After all, if not me, then who?

Carolyn Ray, CEO and Editor, JourneyWoman

While reading Tracey's book, I was constantly presented with the opportunity to reflect on being an outlier for 18 years. I was a Black female in an environment dominated by white men. My company at the time struggled greatly in human resources. Upper management would turn you into a target of condescension; you had to fix the problem of not "fitting in." I wish *Match-Striking for Beginners* had been available when I became an executive with the power to change things. I would have incorporated it into our training program; it would have resulted in a safer, more understanding environment for all. Tracey's book is filled with powerful lessons that can be successfully applied across many workplace environments. For instance, education would benefit from the concepts Tracey presents, welcoming the fact all children are different so shouldn't be taught alike. *Match-Striking for Beginners* is a compelling book that will take those that are narrow-minded to open-minded, provide clarity to those who feel trapped and invisible who feel dismissed, anxious, and frightened, giving them hope that they can change things rather than quit life. Tracey's book lets you know it's okay to be who you are because you are valued and safe.

Carla D. DeBow, Retired Corporate Executive, Middle School Teacher, Diversity Consultant

This book is a powerful reminder that each of us has the potential to spark change. It shows that with passion and determination, even the biggest challenges can be overcome, inspiring us to make a significant impact. An essential read for anyone who dreams of making a positive difference in the world.

Pamela Zaballa, Chief Executive Officer, NO MORE

ACTIVATING INDIVIDUAL AND COLLECTIVE **POWER** FOR A MORE JUST WORLD

MATCH-STRIKING
for **BEGINNNERS**
TRACEY BREEDEN

First published in Great Britain by Practical Inspiration Publishing, 2024

© Tracey Breeden, 2024

The moral rights of the author have been asserted.

ISBN   9781788606103 (hardback)
         9781788606110 (paperback)
         9781788606134 (epub)
         9781788606127 (mobi)

Every effort has been made to trace copyright holders and to obtain their permission for the use of copyright material. The publisher apologizes for any errors or omissions and would be grateful if notified of any corrections that should be incorporated in future reprints or editions of this book.

Want to bulk-buy copies of this book for your team and colleagues? We can customize the content and co-brand *Match-Striking for Beginners* to suit your business's needs.

Please email info@practicalinspiration.com for more details.

Practical Inspiration
Publishing

Dedication

This book is dedicated to my superhero nieces
Portia and Paris.

May you find your pathway to hope, healing,
purpose, and personal power.

Contents

Foreword

Can one person change the world? Am I changemaker material? Many of us who have had the privilege of working in a cause we love sometimes struggle with this question. The issue might seem too big, or you might believe that you are too insignificant to create a lasting impact. You might be weary and questioning your direction until a moment arrives when you are vividly reminded that every single step of the way is worth it and that you indeed have what it takes.

One of those pivotal moments for me was the day Tracey and I spoke to an audience about the impact of sexual violence. It was by no means an easy conversation. She and I came from different backgrounds, each with our unique stories. I led a non-governmental organization (NGO) on the topic, and she worked for a big tech firm. That was enough to assume that I was there to start a revolution and that her role was to be measured and corporate. However, the opposite was about to happen. I found a deep connection in every one of her words, and the energy that moved her had a direct, resonating impact on what I was saying too. I had found a kindred spirit in advocacy that day. Her conviction, passion, and structured vision for changing the landscape was something I had struggled to ever find in my own sector. Never would I have imagined seeing that come from a global corporation.

If her personality and experience were not already convincing enough, I was in complete awe at seeing how the audience was reacting. They were not only listening to every word, but they were also living it, feeling every emotion conveyed. Afterwards, many came to talk to us, but in reality, they just wanted to hug her, drawn by the magnetic power of her words and presence. That day I learned one of the most xiv Match-Striking for Beginners

valuable lessons of my career: Your best tool to be a change-maker is your passion, and Tracey had found a way to translate her passion into action that has helped millions.

After that day, we literally traveled the world, and it did not matter whether it was Hyderabad, London, Johannesburg, or Paris—the reaction was the same. The audiences were inspired to execute changes themselves. It is still gratifying for me to hear how many of those teams have developed life-changing projects for many, tackling not only sexual violence but also gender inequality and LGBTQ+ rights and visibility. These projects have sparked a ripple effect of change, touching lives far beyond the immediate scope of our talks.

Fortunately, my time with Tracey taught me that it doesn't matter where or how you start your journey. Activism is a muscle that needs to be felt, cultivated, and exercised. It grows stronger with every action, every word, and every heart you touch.

The answer is YES; you can change the world, your community, your company, or whatever your heart desires. If you are passionate about a cause because it breaks your heart, and you do not let self-doubt win the battle, you will become an icon for others who share your conviction. This book will help you start your journey or reassure you that you are on the right path.

I am glad that many more people will have the ability to feel Tracey's influence and guidance through its pages.

Good luck on your journey!

Pamela Zaballa, CEO, NO MORE Foundation

Introduction: For it is not the light that is needed, but fire...

"For it is not the light that is needed, but fire…"

Frederick Douglass, July 5, 1852

As I reflect back on my life, there are pivotal moments—moments that activated movement for me. Moments that ignited change. Those moments are some of the most vivid memories I have. Moments that cultivated my journey to self, purpose, and my personal power. Moments where I felt I was enough to make a difference.

One of those moments occurred when I was around 12 or 13 years old. It was a time in my life where I was grappling with my sexuality, and not feeling comfortable with the norms and expectations that had been placed upon me. I was Queer and I felt different from most people around me. I felt alone in who I was.

My parents had taken me and my sisters to a park in a neighboring small town. It was the fourth of July, and like many others across middle America, we were celebrating freedom. Yet, I did not feel free to be me. There were many people and lots of activity in the park. Events and activities like carnival games, cook-outs, and pony-rides. There was also a stage where people dressed up as American historical figures delivering famous historical speeches. Historical figures like Abraham Lincoln, George Washington, and Thomas Jefferson. I sat alone near the front and listened.

Then a man, dressed as a historical figure that I had never heard of before, took to the stage. He was a Black man portraying Fredrick Douglass. He was the only Black person I saw in the park that day. I grew up in a small town in northeastern Oklahoma in the U.S., which was predominantly Caucasian and Native American.

From the moment he came on stage, you could feel the passion in his presence alone. He then looked across the crowd and began to speak the words of Fredrick Douglass. You could feel the energy and it gave me chills. The speech, "What to the slave is the fourth of July?" or sometimes called "The fifth of July speech," was delivered by Fredrick Douglass to an antislavery women's group on July 5, 1852.[1]

You could feel the strength and fire in every word he spoke. The speaker didn't read it. He knew and embraced every word by heart. He quickly captured the full attention of nearly every person sitting in the crowd; others who were walking nearby stopped to listen. It was the most powerful speech and the most powerful speaker I had ever heard. I had never observed anything like it, and I have never forgotten that moment.

It impacted me in ways I can't fully describe, but I'll try to explain. It ignited something within me. It sparked a desire for knowledge to learn more about the civil rights movements and about women's movements. It sparked a desire in me to learn more about the Black community, their experiences, and their history.

It also touched something deeply personal in me, connected to who I was and what I felt in every core of my being. I had grown up in a community where I was different and where many people and institutions did not fully acknowledge or value Queer people; these people did not believe that Queer people deserved respect in being fully who they are or that they deserved equal rights. In fact, the common belief was that we only had one destiny, and that was hell. I did not feel free and safe being me.

But on that day, I felt safe, encouraged, and hopeful in those moments during the speech. I felt a human connection with the speaker portraying Frederick Douglass and a connection with the message he was giving and many of the words he delivered that spoke to ALL people deserving the right to freedom, respect, and equality. I felt safe in the presence of the speaker who was also different from the crowd. I didn't feel any energy of fear coming from him. He was fearless. I felt his energy of strength, confidence, and hope. That speech and the person who delivered it ignited a fire in me. It ignited in me hope for change and hope for equality and the experience of respect and freedom I and every human deserve.

After he finished telling the history of the speech and the extraordinary impact Fredrick Douglass had as an educator, activist, abolitionist, writer, and speaker, fighting for social justice and equality, he walked off the stage, made eye contact with me and smiled. I was still in awe, looking at him like he was a superhero. I felt seen even though this person had no idea who I was. It was a moment where I felt valued and thought that maybe I can do this too. It ignited in me a passion and dream of helping others someday who were different, even though I had no idea where my journey would take me.

That moment, that speech, would help to galvanize me and my eventual approach to empowering and creating safe spaces for others like me in the spaces where I lived and worked. That approach would eventually become grounded in a belief that when you empower and create safety for the marginalized, you create safety for everyone.

When I talk about creating safe spaces, I'm not just talking about physical safety. To create social change and safe spaces for women, the LGBTQ+ community, and other marginalized groups, we must not only create an environment of physical safety but also one of emotional and psychological safety. This is when people feel accepted and respected. It is the freedom to be one's true self, and the feeling and belief that you can share who you are, including your thoughts and opinions, without fear of negative consequences. When we have emotional safety within ourselves, there is then a willingness and courage to act, and to express our authentic selves. When we elevate, empower, and prioritize the safety of women, the LGBTQ+ community, the Black community, the Indigenous community, all people of color, people with disabilities, and other historically marginalized groups, it creates safety for not only each of us as individuals but for all people and all communities. It builds authentic, equitable, and respectful communities, free from harm. For me, it became a vision and a mission. It became a vision directly connected to my purpose that goes everywhere I go. No matter the place of work. No matter the platform. No matter who I lead. No matter who I coach or advise.

Practically every day when I wake up, I think about that vision and the need for social change. I think about the expansion of that vision, empowering and igniting people to be better, more powerful versions of themselves, where they recognize, embrace, and unleash their personal power to achieve the desires of their hearts while also joining others to collectively create a better world. Maybe you think about it too or you are starting to think about it more?

This vision is my vision, but it has become the shared vision of so many others. It can be your vision too. It is grounded in the shared value of putting people first through acts of genuine care, because ALL people deserve the right to be safe and free from all forms of harm.

I deeply care about people, and I know I am not alone. I know I'm not alone when I close my eyes, and I see a rainbow of colors. I see what the world could be. I see opportunity. I wake up most days standing in a place of hope even though many days bring difficulty and hopelessness for so many—so many who have a lot in common with me. WE are women, members of the LGBTQ+ community, the Black community, the Indigenous community, all people of color, people with disabilities, and other historically marginalized groups.

Marginalization is also intersectional. Civil rights advocate Kimberlé Crenshaw introduced the theory of intersectionality: "A lens through which you can see where power comes and collides, where it interlocks and intersects. It's not simply that there's a race problem here, a gender problem there, and a class, or LGBTQ+ problem there. Many times that framework erases what happens to people who are subject to all of these things."[2]

During our lives, many of us face discrimination and disadvantages connected to our overlapping and intersecting identities and experiences. In addition, so many people even with the best intentions, including leaders, other professionals, and authors, don't recognize or take into account the additional barriers and difficulties we face on our journey to self-discovery, purpose, and personal power. They sometimes make it sound easy, but the reality is that our journey is hard; it is different, and it is not always safe.

I believe individual and social change needs to happen because people like me and you, and members of so many historically marginalized groups, continue to be harmed. The facts don't lie. Harm continues to happen to people— to the most marginalized in our communities. Each group and individual have unique experiences, but harm also may look similar across groups and regions. We have a long history of experiencing personal and systemic harm and being impacted by barriers, but yet many of us continue to rise up every day, every morning with hope and passion on a mission to find ways to our personal and collective power for individual and social change. We need more people to join us in leading the change we want. We have the power to do it.

Being Queer and being a woman, I know the difficulty all too well myself. Not just from my personal, lived experience but also from my professional experience in public safety, as a leader and executive in the tech industry, as a life coach, advisor, and activist. I know firsthand the lived experiences and stories of so many who I have responded to, who I have helped, who have sat in front of me and told me the stories of the best, but also the worst, days of their lives.

The majority of people who have sat in front of me, who have experienced the most severe forms of harm, were indeed women, members of the LGBTQ+ community, people of color, and other historically marginalized groups. For it is the most marginalized in our communities that are the most adversely impacted by harassment, hate, and harm. Their stories I carry with me. Stories that will never leave me. They are more than just numbers and statistics. They are human beings with real human experiences of harm and their experiences span the globe. No community is immune.

Perhaps you will be surprised to learn that I was a police officer for a number of years, and you will hear me reference some of my experiences in this book during my time in law enforcement. Before I share those stories, it's important that I acknowledge the institutional racism, misogyny, and homophobia that exists in law enforcement in the U.S. and across the world. Law enforcement has greatly harmed and failed many in historically marginalized communities. It is a system like many others that has deeply rooted, systemic problems that have not been adequately addressed and need further change and accountability from a human rights-centered approach.

I often found myself personally conflicted in choosing the profession of policing as a Queer woman. It wasn't always easy and there were many frustrating experiences for me, but my heart called me to it and that is where I first found purpose and power in what broke my heart, in my community, serving alongside others. As a police officer, I personally made a commitment to never stand by when I saw people being harmed, no matter who was doing the harm. There were many others who honored that commitment with me, and I worked alongside some extraordinary human beings who were dedicated to serving and protecting all people from a place of integrity and genuine care. I have the heart of a public servant, and that is what a public servant does. You don't have to be a police officer to be a public servant. No matter the profession, community, or institution, you too can be a public servant for all people by upholding these shared values.

My story is the message of my heart, and it is weaved into this book. For it is in what broke my heart that I found my purpose and personal power to become fully and authentically me. I rose up to stand in a place of hope and courage, embracing my vision and mission. I unleashed the superhero within me. I chose disruption and freedom. I still choose it every day and stand for myself, the most marginalized, and those who are seeking to rise into personal and collective power for a more just world.

Before founding my own coaching and consulting practice in 2023, I spent almost 15 years working in law enforcement prioritizing the most vulnerable in our communities before landing in tech companies to lead and develop efforts in safety, inclusion, and social advocacy, including many industry firsts. I found success and fulfillment in my personal journey and professionally on the inside of tech companies weaving mission-driven work into my day job after igniting my personal power while in law enforcement. I would soon find myself as the first Head of Women's Safety and Gender-Based Violence at the rideshare giant Uber, and then eventually the first Vice President, Head of Safety and Social Advocacy for Match Group. Match Group is the largest online dating company with a global app portfolio including Tinder, Hinge, and OkCupid.

Recognizing my personal power and unleashing the superhero within me while I was a police officer took me on a journey of becoming fully who I am, achieving the desires of my heart and making an impactful difference in the world, individually and collectively, with others who joined and helped me. I'll tell you how I did it, and I'll also share stories of others I know personally. I have permission to share

xxii Match-Striking for Beginners

their stories, but some of the names have been changed and details omitted to protect their privacy.

Creating change, community, movement, and the path to execution was not simple or easy. In fact, it was hard. Really hard at times. You won't be surprised by that if you are a woman, a member of the LGBTQ+ community, or another historically marginalized group. We know hard, and our hearts continue to break in this unjust world.

But, let me encourage you that there is hope and there is a pathway to igniting big change and movement, both personally and collectively. I learned some valuable insights along my journey about myself, others, and systems that I believe are critical to activating your personal power and then collective power with others towards the bold, disruptive change we need individually, while also creating the better, more just world that we all want, that our hearts ache for. I'll offer deep insight and the step-by-step method I employed to unleash my own personal power and inner superhero to achieve remarkable success in creating change, and I invite you to ignite your power from the margin.

As you read this book, you may notice some repetition of words and similar phrases referencing your personal power, your purpose, and what's breaking your heart, unleashing your inner superhero and reminding you that you are enough to create change. Why? Because the messages that we are not good enough, we are not deserving, and we do not have power are messages we see and hear over and over again as women and members of marginalized groups. Those limiting, harmful messages are weaved into our culture and experiences. They have caused harm and slowed progress. I repeat words and phrases purposefully in this book as mantras to release positive energy and thoughts and help focus and ground you in what is true. There is power in what is true. I'm on a mission to disrupt the harmful, limiting thoughts and messages thereby helping you ignite your personal power.

This book is for women, members of the LGBTQ+ community, and other historically marginalized groups. This book is about hope, resilience, human connection, leadership, and change. My hope is that you will be inspired and empowered in the spaces where you live and work to ignite personal change and collective social change. I believe change starts first with self—with you, individually—before you can join together with others to have meaningful impact collectively. It's time to unleash more superheroes. You may not believe it, but you are a superhero. I wrote this book so that you would not only feel seen but also to help you see you are enough to create change.

This is also a book for those of you who are already changemakers far along your journey of self-discovery, purpose, and personal power. No matter how far along that path you are, you still need encouragement, inspiration, hope, and a reminder that you are not alone. Sometimes you need more tools in your toolbox. Sometimes superheroes need to be reignited to continue to create meaningful and sustainable change.

All people deserve safe, respectful, and equitable spaces and experiences. We need big, bold, disruptive social change to ensure that we get what we deserve. We all have a responsibility and role to play when harm is happening to our communities. Let me help you identify and find your match-striking opportunities and role and show you a pathway to igniting your personal power and unleashing the superhero inside of you.

The moment that superhero fire and power in you is ignited you will find you are not alone. You were never alone. When you recognize and embrace that you too are a superhero, then, together, we can all ignite a fire that can bring about the change we dream of.

You are enough

A journey of rejection

You are enough. Let me say that again. You are enough. You have the personal power within you to be fully and authentically who you are and have the desires of your heart, while also making an impactful difference in the world. You are enough to create change.

I know there are moments and days when you don't believe you are enough. In fact, the days you don't believe may greatly outnumber the days you do. I ask you to hold on to the belief you are enough for the time that it takes you to finish this book, and then tell me what you believe.

I know it's hard to believe when you have been wounded and faced rejection time and time again. For women, the LGBTQ+ community, the Black community, the Indigenous community, all people of color, people with disabilities, and other historically marginalized groups, it has been a journey of rejection at too many turns to count, micro and macro. You can be overwhelmed at times with the enormous challenges as members of these groups. I know you're tired—sometimes you are so tired of fighting the fight that it's hard to maintain hope. It's hard to believe that things will ever change. It's hard to know what to do at times. It's difficult to understand why harm continues. This is my lived experience too.

The truth is we have been rejected and silenced for centuries, and it has adversely impacted our progress. Rejection comes in many forms. Rejection comes in the form of stereotypes and culturally held beliefs that start to impact us early on. If we don't live up to those cultural beliefs and stereotypes, if we don't fulfill the expectations, we are rejected.

Rejection can be implicit or explicit. When we experience prejudice and stigmatization, we are rejected. When we are excluded and treated unjustly for our race, ethnicity, nationality, religion, disability, gender or sexual orientation—for just being who we are—we are rejected. When we are treated unfairly and disrespectfully, we are rejected. This rejection adversely impacts our relationship with self and our relationship with others. Achieving a sense of acceptance and belonging is necessary for our psychological and physical well-being and safety. When our need for acceptance and belonging is not satisfied, there are negative, immediate effects and long-term effects on our health.[1]

Often from our earliest days, we are molded into what society and others think we should be. And if we start to define ourselves outside of acceptable social norms we are told we are wrong or that we shouldn't feel, act, or be the way that feels authentic to us. Our authenticity is rejected. This rejection shows up in the form of words, lack of opportunities, and in the expectations laid upon us by individuals and society. This rejection comes in the form of exclusion rather than inclusion.

I recall growing up Queer in middle America and never feeling like I fitted in. I never fitted in as a child or as a teen. I was told that, as a girl and woman, I should look a certain way, from the way I wore my hair, to how I acted, and how I dressed. I hated going clothes shopping for school. I was called a tomboy and was ridiculed. I didn't always want to wear girls' clothes. I wanted to wear boys' clothes too. I spent time trying to find the least feminine thing I could find in the girls' section of clothing stores. I am incredibly thankful for the moment that I found Calvin Klein in college! That was a game changer for me.

The gender-conforming expectations I was under, like so many others, were damaging to my self-esteem and self-respect. My understanding of femininity and masculinity was informed by the culture I was a part of, influenced by both cultural misinformation and disinformation.

I struggled with my relationship with self and did not recognize my own personal power. Being fully me, being Queer, was not accepted and was not considered normal. I played sports because it gave me permission to feel what it was like to be me, to be something more than what was traditionally expected of a woman. Even though sport was more often than not associated with men, women were allowed to also play certain sports. Even today, we still don't always get the same recognition. How many times have we heard that word "allowed!" I remember working so hard and putting so much energy into trying to fit into the stereotypes and cultural norms that were placed upon me in my youth, but at the same time wanting and trying to just be me.

In being me, rejection came in the form of erroneous beliefs, language, and behavioral responses from family, friends, institutions, and society. Responses and attitudes that did not create spaces that felt safe, empowering, and affirming. I felt powerless and had no hope things could change.

As a Queer person, rejection showed up for me in educational settings, churches, and at nearly every turn. Even as a Queer female police officer, I frequently not only heard but perceived through the actions of others that people like me did not belong. I so deeply desired to serve the public and my community, but I was acutely aware of gender disparities, stereotypes, and a seemingly never-ending misogynistic culture. In fact, from the moment I began the process to become a police officer, I became aware of the attitudes and inequities that were present.

Women police officers report that they experience bias, sexual and racial harassment, and an underestimation of their physical abilities, as well as feeling less influential than their male colleagues. Overall, nearly half of women police officers report discrimination and prejudice based on their gender.[2] And those are the ones that feel safe to report this.

Figures are underreported and numbers are higher in certain regions. I will reference some of my personal experiences in law enforcement in this book. It's important that I acknowledge the institutional racism, misogyny, and homophobia that exists in law enforcement in the U.S. and across the world. As I said in my introduction, law enforcement has greatly harmed and failed many in historically marginalized communities. It is a system like many others that has deeply rooted, systemic problems that have not been adequately addressed and need further change and accountability from a human rights-centered approach.

I was a law enforcement officer in several U.S. regions, both conservative and liberal, and inequities, harassment, and discrimination showed up in all of them. I began my public safety career in the San Francisco Bay area and closed out my career in Arizona before transitioning to the world of tech. I'll never forget my first week on the job when I transferred to a Phoenix suburb. During those first weeks on the job, I went to a domestic violence call, which is a daily occurrence in law enforcement.

In this case, an ex-husband had showed up at his ex-wife's home unannounced. She had a protective order, and family members immediately called the police. He was drunk and was violently threatening her, beating on her front door. I took the lead on the call, showed up on scene with backup, and took the ex-husband into custody at the front door. While officers were finishing up final interviews, and I was finishing up my initial paperwork sitting in my patrol car with the suspect secured in the back, I was unaware that another officer and his partner had shown up on scene. The officer decided to enter the survivor/victim's home and search her entire home.

He conducted an unreasonable search and seizure of people and property inside the home, including detaining the family member that originally called the police for help, after he found a small amount of marijuana on this family member's person. The victim and family inside the home were justifiably upset by the treatment they received from the officer. The family member he placed under arrest had been instrumental in attempting to calm the suspect and keep him away from the victim until the police arrived.

The officer came out of the house with a small bag of marijuana and a marijuana pipe that he found in a bedroom dresser drawer. Small amounts of recreational marijuana were not legal in Arizona at the time and arrests for this type of offense had a disproportionate impact on marginalized communities.

"I searched the house and found this for you," he told me as he stopped at my car window. He threw the bag of marijuana and the pipe on my dashboard and gestured toward the family member standing with his partner in handcuffs. "I know sometimes women need help doing the job. I took care of this one for you," he said with a smirk. "I'll even do the arrest paperwork for you."

I won't use the same language here that I used with him that day but suffice to say I threw the bag of marijuana and pipe on the ground at his feet, told him to wipe the smile off his face, and tore up his paperwork. Then I firmly outlined to him that his behavior and actions were inappropriate, against policy, and were a violation of rights.

"Take that marijuana and pipe and dispose of it. Then get off my scene and don't ever come back. In fact, don't ever show up on any of my scenes again or provide me back up," I told him. I have no tolerance for unethical behavior and people. "And one last thing," I said, "I don't need any man doing the job for me. I guess it took a woman to tell you how to do your job right." He didn't say another word and left my scene.

I took the family member out of handcuffs, apologized to the victim and her family, and encouraged them to file a complaint. Later that evening, after I got out of booking at the jail, the lieutenant leading the district that evening asked me to meet him in a parking lot to talk. When I pulled up, he rolled down his window and told me what he had heard about what had happened on my scene.

It had gotten around to him quickly what had happened and how I had responded. "What happened?" my lieutenant asked me. I responded confidently without hesitation, detailing for him exactly what happened and exactly how I responded. I also shared with him my values and in turn the expectations I had of the officers who worked with me. "You are exactly what we need," he told me, smiling. I smiled back at him as he said, "Good job, Breeden. I like you. In working with me, you will find I share those same values. Thank you for being a role model for other officers. You have my support."

My lieutenant told me he would make certain the officer was held accountable. He did exactly what he said, and also reached out to the family that had been impacted. In that moment, he was a role model for me and others, and it was a privilege for me to work alongside him. He always stood for what was right, including investing in and supporting women in law enforcement. As for the officer who showed up on my scene that day, he never showed up again on any of the scenes I was leading. He eventually lost his job and certification as a police officer for misconduct and abuse of power.

I've rarely, if ever, engaged with a woman, a member of the LGBTQ+ community, or other marginalized group that has not been silenced or experienced some form of rejection along their journey. Now some may say all people have experienced rejection, but the reality is the rejection we face is rooted in systemic inequity, harassment, violence, and discrimination.

I am deeply grateful to the cisgender male allies who have supported me and so many others who have fought to disrupt and dismantle the systems that have oppressed us. But there is much more to do, and we must lead the change. It is our lived experiences and we— women, the LGBTQ+

community, and other marginalized groups—must lead the change we want in our own personal lives and in the world around us.

In the story I shared, I did not deserve, nor did I have to accept, the rejection that came from that police officer who showed up on my scene, and neither did the family we were sent there to protect. I refused to allow it in my space, on my watch. But I didn't always believe I was enough to do that, and that wasn't always my story. One of the main takeaways I want you to leave with from these two stories in this chapter is that in the second one my personal power was ignited. My inner superhero was unleashed.

Change starts with self. Begin by fully acknowledging you have been rejected and that rejection is not your fault. You are not deserving of rejection for who you are. You won't be able to believe you are enough to create the change you want personally or in society until you first stop rejecting yourself. We reject ourselves when we believe the lies, when we stand by and remain silent, when we believe we are not enough, and when we choose not to be true to ourselves.

Rejection hurts, it silences people, it harms people, and it has a real adverse impact on women and marginalized groups, but we can persevere and overcome its damage. Become aware of the systemic lies that exist in rejection and begin to push back on it by disrupting it with what is true. Work towards fully accepting yourself, remembering that you have the personal power within you. We are enough and the power is within us to be fully who we are to create the change we want to see.

You have value

You begin to recognize and activate your personal power to create individual and social change when you realize and fully embrace this truth—you have value. You can bring your value to any situation. You have beauty, skills, and abilities, some that are uniquely your own that differentiate you from everyone else in the world. That's how special you are. Nobody else has your lived experiences, your story, your light, or your personal power. Nobody but you.

There is value in just being who you are, choosing to care, and showing up with genuine and consistent actions. I promise you that will be more than enough to create the change you want. You must recognize your own value and make peace with yourself before you can fully see the value in creating change for yourself and others. You are a powerful force.

I'm a huge fan of the Marvel movies. I've seen nearly all of them! I embrace the meaning behind the group of superheroes called the Avengers. I love helping people see that they too can be superheroes. That they alone have special skills and abilities that can help make the desires of their heart a reality while also making a difference in their community and in the world. You may not see it yet, but I believe there is a superhero within you waiting to be unleashed!

If you are familiar with the Marvel series, you will know the stories and meaning behind the characters. The characters are ordinary, flawed people who are far from perfect. The Marvel characters are people stigmatized for race, ethnic identity, sexual orientation, and even immigrant status. They struggle with personal and social issues. They struggle with self-acceptance, finding their true selves, and realizing their true potential. They all have within them unique superpowers. They represent the hope and power that we all have within us to stand for what is right and create change. One of my very favorite quotes is from Frigga in *Avengers Endgame*:

"Everyone fails at who they are supposed to be, Thor. The measure of a person, of a hero... is how well they succeed at being who they are."[3]

I always refer to my teams and people I work with as superheroes. When people go to work for me, or I'm in a position of coaching or supporting them, I ask them to choose a superhero they most relate to, and that becomes their nickname. I've also used all-star athletes in the past. It has been inspiring for most of them, because if they haven't embraced it already, it helps them begin to believe in their inner superhero. Their superhero and nickname become a symbol of encouragement for them. I want it to be a continual reminder to them that they have value and the personal power to make a difference in who they are. They bring individual talents, skills, and abilities. When they look around, I want them to know they are not alone. Together, when we assemble, we have the collective power to drive positive change. We can be unstoppable.

My superhero character is Captain America. Some of my team members chose it for me as their leader. I always wanted Captain America to be Queer woman! It seems right to have a Queer woman as one of the leaders and superheroes involved in changing the world! However, I didn't always see the superhero within me.

I didn't always believe I had value. Once I did, everything changed for me as I began to see my own personal power and recognize my own value. This is my story of how I found value in being me. It was one of the pivotal points in my life that helped to bring me to where I am today.

I grew up in rural, northeastern Oklahoma on a ranch. I grew up in a loving family with parents and two sisters, but I also grew up in a culture that was not accepting of who I was. For both my parents, religion was very influential in their lives. Once my father became an adult and began his own journey, he rejected many of the beliefs and expectations of the religion within which he was raised. My mother held on to many of her Southern Baptist roots, particularly in my early childhood. We were taken to church regularly and encouraged to uphold many of the traditionally held beliefs of the church. I was right in the middle of what is referred to as the "Bible Belt" in the U.S.

There were many expectations in the culture I grew up in, including beliefs around what women were supposed to be and do. Women were expected to fall in love and find a husband, get married, and have a family. Being gay was considered an abomination and hell and misery was your only destination.

I was surrounded by traditional stereotypes and religious beliefs that were placed on me, that were placed upon my mother and father and those who came before us. It put a lot of pressure on me starting early in my youth. When I was young I knew I was gay from an early age. My misery didn't come from being gay. It came from hiding it. There was no one to talk to about my gender or my sexual orientation. There was no safe space that had been created for any of that.

I lived in fear and put all my energy into being what society and culture expected me to be. I worked very hard to do what I was supposed to do—what I was told I should do. I definitely succeeded at that. I worked hard at it. In addition to being everything I was told a woman should be, I excelled in school, I excelled at sports, and I was the only one in my immediate family to attend and graduate from college. In college, I met my soon-to-be husband.

That was over 30 years ago. When I tell people who didn't know me then that I was married to a man, they are shocked. People who know me have a hard time believing it! I know you probably looked at my picture in my book or you've looked me up on the web and you're like seriously, you were married to a man!

Yes, I was. Not that we should ever make judgments about someone's sexual orientation, but mine is not hard to guess because I went from being very closeted to being very public and out. When people give me that look of shock and awe, I usually shrug my shoulders and say he had very feminine energy, which is true! It will come as no surprise to you that

I preferred men who had strong feminine energy while I was closeted.

Being with a woman went against everything I was told and presented with as being acceptable even though deep inside I knew exactly what I wanted. I did what I was supposed to do, and I got married when I was 21 right before going to graduate school. We got married in a church, I attended graduate school at a Christian university, and I remained married throughout my twenties. My husband was like my best friend, but the mask I was wearing was suffocating me. It was all a show. We were involved in the church. We had outwardly similar married friends. I worked very hard to look happy, to look like life was good, but inside I was suffering. My desire and attraction for women was intense, and my desire to be my authentic self was intense, but I never talked about my true feelings to anyone.

I would carefully and outwardly support the LGBTQ+ community, but not too loudly for fear I might be rejected or outed. It was okay for others to be gay, but it was not okay for me. I was working so hard to be something I was not, and I didn't see any value in being me—fully and completely me. I felt tremendous shame and guilt. I was exhausted from all the energy I put into being someone I was not.

During my marriage, the suffering continued to escalate. That internal suffering lasted for over ten years. Then in my early thirties, I lost my father. He died way too early and unexpectedly. I was close to my father, and it felt like a part of my heart had been ripped out when he died. He was one of the most important people in my life who saw through the front I was putting up. I knew he was aware I was gay. He never had to say it out loud.

He called me Trace. "Trace," he would always ask me, "are you sure you're happy? It just seems like there's something you're deeply struggling with..." I couldn't lie to his face and say I was happy, so I would look away when I said, "I can't talk about it. I'll be fine." When I would sometimes introduce him to female friends, he would later make it a point to tell me he liked them and that he thought they were cute with a grin on his face. Not in a creepy way, but in a way a father affirms his child and their choices. It was exactly clear what he meant.

I believe he always knew I was gay even in my youth. Now that I look back, I can tell even more by the many things he did to affirm who I was. He was always supportive of me no matter what, and I truly believe he would have been supportive of me being authentic and fully who I am because that's what he modeled for me.

It was my father's death and working as a police officer that helped me see how short life is and how it can be taken so abruptly. It made me stop in my tracks and seek more out of life. I wanted freedom and life fully being me. My father's death made me think about my own life differently. My desire to live my truth intensified greatly during that time.

I wanted to come-out from my secrecy—from living an inauthentic life. I wanted to leave my marriage. But I hesitated. I told myself that even though doing so would bring me joy, it would cause hurt for so many others. It meant walking away from a life I had created with another person. It meant disappointing family, friends, and failing at the expectations I was working so hard to maintain.

All I could think about was the potential negative impact, not the positive. My head was full of everything that could go wrong. I knew many family members and friends would also not approve, and I knew it would break my husband's heart. But the truth was I was continuing to break my own heart over and over again by choosing to not embrace and value myself for who I was. The decision was beyond difficult. I spent nights crying in agony over the decision. I spent my days trying to escape it. I questioned whether life was even worth living.

The week after my father died, I remember sitting on my bed one night in such deep pain contemplating whether life was worth living. I had just got home from work as a police officer, and I was sitting there with my police service weapon. The same gun I carried on duty. I held it in my lap and stared at it in deep pain as tears ran down my face. I had made the decision to take my life and end the pain and agony for myself. I remember reaching down and grasping the handle of the gun.

As I began to raise it, something made me pause. I was faced with two choices. I could either take my life or I could choose to live life. I wanted life, but if I was going to choose to live I had to live it as my full, authentic self. I could no longer live a lie. My head was suddenly flooded with thoughts and voices of strength and courage I had heard before, calling me and pressing me to rise up and live for me.

The time was now to put myself first and give myself the life I deserved—being the real me. I started to believe I could do it, and I should not waste another second of my life. I embraced in that moment, how valuable my life was, and I was not willing to sacrifice it any longer. In that moment I chose me, and that choice gave me life and freedom.

That pivotal moment I chose life was the moment I also chose to start valuing myself, putting myself first. It was a spark that kicked off a journey of self-awareness, self-acceptance, and self-power. I would soon after be divorced, publicly out, and starting what felt like a new life. Beginning to recognize my personal power by standing up for myself first, by valuing myself first and embracing my better, true self, was the pathway to unleashing the superhero within me.

You will hear more stories about my personal journey as well as others. The impactful change and remarkable success I drove in my own life helped me be a driven leader in tech companies like Uber and in policing, and most importantly in other people's lives. This would never have happened had I not first chosen to value myself and embrace my personal power.

Over time and with help, I started to recognize and embrace that I too could be a superhero, and manifest and make real the desires of my heart while creating spaces to help drive positive change not only in myself but also in the world. However, it first took me putting my energy into just being me rather than putting energy into being what society and those around me expected me to be. The amount of energy I put into those expectations didn't allow space for me to be able to be truly and authentically me while also investing in other people's lives and in this world.

Your story won't be the same as mine. You may not be gay, but you may be hiding who you are and what you want in a closet. The expectations don't have to look exactly the same. Your identity may look different. You have your own story and journey. Let me tell you that you being fully you is enough. You have your own skills, abilities, and personal power to make a difference in your own life and in this world. You first have to recognize your value and show up for yourself in the moments this life gives you before you can authentically show up for others.

Hold on to hope even if you're tired and overwhelmed by your own lived experience and in society across the world. I'll share with you how I, along with others, have found ways to manifest the desires of our hearts, while also creating safe spaces and driving positive impact from being just who we are.

Did you know you have a superhero within you waiting to be unleashed? I believe that within you there is the ability to create the change you want to see in just being who you are. You need you. Your community needs you. The world needs you to value yourself and recognize you too are a superhero. See yourself for who you truly are and embrace the personal power that lives within you.

You are enough to create change. Believe it.

Chapter 1 activators

✺ **Reflection questions**:

➤➤ How does my own experience of rejection influence my self-view?

➤➤ Stand in front of a mirror and say out loud, "I have value." What emotions do you feel? What do you feel in your body? What thoughts do you have in response?

✺ **Personal power tip**: Speak out loud to yourself. Talk to yourself. Hear yourself talk. Do it in front of a mirror. Do it during meditation. Get comfortable with saying positive things about yourself, what is true, what you want, and what you believe. It was once very difficult and uncomfortable for me to do that. It's okay, we all feel that discomfort at times. That is why we must make it a continual personal power practice. With practice and persistence, it will become comfortable. It will become powerful. When you can say these things to yourself out loud with courage and confidence, you will then be able to consistently say them out loud in front of others during the most difficult and uncomfortable times. It begins with self.

✺ **Unleash your superhero**: What superhero characters do you most relate to? Research superheroes, their personal powers, their struggles, and their personality traits. Which ones do you most relate to? What about them inspires and connects with you?

✺ **Manifestation affirmation**: I have value in being me. I prioritize myself and put my energy into just being me rather than putting energy into being what society and those around me expect me to be.

Disrupt the limiting voices and thoughts

The voice that says you are not enough may never go away

How many times have you heard you need to identify your limiting thoughts and beliefs and then work to eliminate and stop them? There are many so-called solutions out there you can spend lots of money on that tell you exactly that and keep you coming back. Apparently, it's all on you to make them stop and, as a result, there is something wrong with you if they continue. I'm going to call it what it is and tell you that it's a lie that keeps you from igniting your personal power to become fully who you are, achieving the desires of your heart, and making an impactful difference in the world, individually and collectively.

As women and other members of under-recognized and marginalized groups, we often hear a limiting voice inside our head that tells us that we're not enough. I mean we've heard it from society. We hear those limiting messages at every turn. We hear them in our workplaces. We hear them at home. Maybe it's not always those exact words, "you are not enough," but it's similar language and actions that deliver that message.

Maybe we deliver the limiting messages to ourselves. No matter the source, the immediate feeling you feel in your body is that you are not enough. By the way, everyday super-heroes hear that limiting voice telling them that they're not enough or not good enough. Yes, I said superheroes hear that voice. Don't let misconceptions around perfect be the enemy of good.

"You are enough."

Don't believe the lie that you have to achieve your perfect, best self to be a superhero. Don't believe that the limiting voice that tells you "You are not enough" will go away. Even after you recognize your limiting thoughts and embrace your value, it will remain. Don't dedicate all your energy and allow your end goal to be the elimination of that voice and those limiting thoughts. It will only lead to disappointment and guilt. It was a lesson I had to learn myself as I became more self-aware.

I'm going to tell you the opposite of what you may believe. I'm going to tell you that you have to accept that limiting voice that tells you at times "you are not enough" will continue to be there. So many people put so much time, money, and energy trying to completely get rid of that voice and those limiting thoughts, that when they show up, they feel like a failure. They feel guilt and shame. We put a tremendous amount of energy and time into removing those limiting voices and thoughts. People may tell us there is something wrong with us if we are still hearing that voice. We even pay them to tell us that!

That energy would be better placed elsewhere. What you focus on is where your energy flows. Energy is powerful. We get caught up in the belief that because that voice of self-doubt is still there telling us we aren't enough, that maybe it is actually true. The limiting voice and thoughts convince us we don't have the personal power or answers within us to become better versions of ourselves and to achieve what we want. It extends to our perceived ability to impact society. It convinces us we are not quite enough to be a superhero, because certainly superheroes don't continue to struggle with those limiting voices and thoughts.

We tell ourselves that the people who have a high level of self-awareness are embracing their personal power and are creating great personal and societal change in this world don't often hear limiting messages in their heads. We believe that even when they go through tough times and moments, they easily shift to an optimistic mindset of positivity and meet the challenge head on. That is not always true, and their struggles are not always regularly shared.

If you have a look at my track record, I've accomplished a lot and driven results. I've been very successful personally and professionally since coming out of the closet, embracing fully who I am, recognizing my personal power, and working on my relationship with myself. I have experienced expansive personal transformation and growth, I've led and influenced people and organizational change in my leadership, executive, and business roles, and I've been able to accomplish big, mission-driven, purposeful work that I could have never dreamed of. It hasn't stopped. I continue to elevate and expand.

Guess what?

I still hear that limiting voice telling me I'm not enough at times. I can't tell you how many times I have even doubted myself while writing this book! You see, you are not alone. It's estimated that 85% of the world's population are affected by some level of low self-worth or self-respect.[1]

Countless upon countless notable activists and champions for change, past and present, struggle with self-doubt. Let me name a few for you: John F. Kennedy, Leonardo De Vinci, George Eliot, Justice Sonia Sotomayor, Maya Angelo, Penelope Cruz, and Candice Carty-Williams. The list goes on and on from celebrities, to change agents, to everyday leaders, and what society would define as successful people.[2, 3]

The former first lady, Michelle Obama, while speaking in London on her book tour, talked about self-doubt. The question "Am I good enough?" continues to impact her even today. "It never goes away," she said. "It's sort of like 'you're actually listening to me?' It doesn't go away, that feeling of 'I don't know if the world should take me seriously; I'm just Michelle Robinson, that little girl on the south side who went to public school.'"[4]

What is true? You must accept and realize that the limiting voice asking you, "Am I good enough?" is going to be there; it's going to live with you, but it doesn't have to stop you from becoming a better version of yourself, making a difference in the world around you and from being the superhero that lives within you. Acceptance is the first step to defeating its power over you. It's okay that you're hearing that voice. Superheroes hear that voice. Stop fighting to make it go completely away and accept it—but don't stop there.

Recognize the trends and strike in the moment

Working in public safety and as a police officer, I learned early on that you first have to identify the trends of harm if you want to successfully address them and create an impact. Otherwise, you may be wasting a lot of time if you don't understand the exact trend of how it's occurring, when it's occurring, and how it may be specifically impacting a person or community.

As you read this, you may be thinking, "How does this story relate to quieting the voice and limiting thoughts that tell me that I'm not enough?" Now, hang in there with me for a moment and I'll explain.

Pretend you are an investigator, like Detective Olivia Benson from the TV show Law and Order. Let's say there is a trend around an increase in home break-ins. If we dig deeper, we might find out that the majority of them are happening in the middle of the day when people are typically not at home and are at work. Maybe the majority are happening between the hours of 3 pm and 4 pm. We might also identify that they're happening within a three-block perimeter, in a particular part of a community near a high school.

Identifying information around trends can help us create a plan to address it that will be most effective. For example, it's helpful to increase patrol in that specific neighborhood during the hours of the most frequent occurrences. The most effective approach would be to create a plan of how to address it by utilizing the information that you gather to help change and reduce the break-ins.

I like to tackle things like an investigator. As a leader and expert, that was the same way I tackled and identified trust, safety, and inclusion issues within the tech industry in which I worked. I led and collaborated with teams to look for trends, both on the platform and in real life, connected to safety and inclusion. For example, in rideshare there were trends around fake rideshare drivers who were assaulting riders. It was learned from police and expert advocacy groups that they were typically occurring in the evening and overnight hours. They were occurring at a higher rate in entertainment districts. Victims were regularly in vulnerable situations such as being intoxicated.

We took a multi-pronged approach to address it in collaboration with businesses, expert advocacy groups, and law enforcement from creating real-time education and awareness campaigns to leveraging technology and safety features. You may not always be able to point to the specific approach that had the greatest impact but collectively taking a multi-faceted approach resulted in a decrease in these types of incidents and improved collaboration.

You might be thinking again, "Tracey, what does addressing trends of harm have to do with limiting voices and thoughts?" Believe me, I don't just like telling cop stories! It's what we can learn from the approach. Identifying trends in any situation helps us effectively reduce impact or harm.

Let's now take a look at the trends around when we have limiting thoughts and when we hear those voices of self-doubt. What type of mindset do they show up in? I know that if I strike and disrupt them in the moment, I'm going to have better success at quieting the voice and moving forward into the action that my intuition and heart are calling me to take that can make a difference for myself and others.

Let's look at the mechanics of how we can most effectively disrupt those limiting thoughts and messages before they land. The first trend that I've recognized with myself and others is the voice telling you that you are not enough intensifies in moments of opportunity. It intensifies when you're at that crossroads of making a decision to act upon what you feel your heart is calling you to do. This might be a situation or moment of opportunity where you're about to do something or create something that could result in meaningful impact. A moment to strike a match that could light a fire igniting personal power!

Maybe you've been thinking about writing a book, taking a stand for yourself, starting a non-profit organization, developing a support program, speaking up on behalf of a colleague who is experiencing inequity, educating a group on human rights, beginning or exiting a relationship with a person or institution, communicating what you deserve, or challenging the status quo. It's in these moments when the universe presents an opportunity for you to act, to show up for yourself, for another person, or for an organization, that the limiting voice comes flooding to the forefront of your mind.

The voice will say many things that try to limit you. "What you do and say won't even matter to them." "Nobody will really care." "It probably won't work." "I'm just this kid who grew up in a small town." "Somebody else can do it better." "They won't listen." "It won't make a difference." "It's just too hard." "The worst could happen." "I'm not 'enough' to make a change." You will hear these limiting voices and thoughts and you will also feel it in your body. Your muscles may become tense. You may feel anxiety. Your breathing will change. You may find yourself holding your breath. Think about what your body does during those moments.

You will sometimes know the exact timing of when the opportunity is going to happen; for example, when I know I am going to have to sit down and work on writing my book on Wednesday. Maybe you have a meeting on your calendar to discuss a promotion, a proposal, or a speaking event to present an important topic. Think about what you can do beforehand to disrupt that voice and those limiting thoughts from stopping you or adversely impacting the important work you feel called to do or the important message you feel called to share. Those will be opportunities that you can plan for, or you can address proactively prior to the event. The limiting thoughts may surface so you need to identify ways to disrupt and quiet them so you can create the right mindset and the right space to be able to move forward with the right action.

But, then there are times that it's more in the moment, that it's unplanned, where it just happens, and you feel that tugging inside of you to act. In that same moment, the voices of self-doubt appear. This is one of the trends that I see with myself and so many others.

I've worked alongside, led, and coached so many people who have come to me with self-doubt; they question their value, and question whether they can make a real impact. In addition to the evidence, I know firsthand that this is a very common struggle and obstacle for women and historically marginalized groups professionally. According to a study by the National Bureau of Economic Research, nearly 80% of women struggle with low self-esteem and avoid self-advocacy at work.[5]

The other trend that I often see is a scarcity mindset. It is rooted in fear and becomes a huge blocker for us when we give it power. I believe one of the greatest teachers on the scarcity mindset is Lynne Twist, a world-renowned author, activist, and founder of The Soul of Money Institute who, for more than 40 years, has been recognized as a global visionary committed to alleviating poverty and hunger and supporting social justice and environmental sustainability.

What is a scarcity mindset? Lynne tells us in her book, *Living a Committed Life*, that there are three toxic myths that create a scarcity mindset and maintain it.[6] I know these will sound familiar to you! The first myth she discusses is *there is not enough*. Believing *there is not enough* cripples us to where we put our energy and focus on what is not true. This is the belief that there are not enough resources for everyone—resources like food, money, and time. It's that feeling that you'll never have enough. It's easy to tell ourselves, "There just aren't enough resources, so I shouldn't bother asking. They're just going to say no. They rarely say yes."

The second toxic myth Lynne discusses is *more is better.* When we believe this, we find that the need for more and more is never ending. It's the belief that we need more money, we need more time, we need a bigger home and space, and we need more and more things. At the core of the belief that we need to accumulate more is the belief that *more is better.* Lynne tells us the pursuit of possessing more and more keeps us distracted from being fulfilled with what we have.

The third toxic myth Lynne discusses is *that's just the way it is.* I don't know how many times I've heard this one in government and corporations! "This is how it has always been," we're told time and again. Or "This is how we have always done it." Lynne tells us it becomes a mantra we adopt with everything we believe we lack the ability to control or the power to change, creating a space of helplessness and hopelessness. I've seen this become ingrained in people's personal lives but also in the culture of organizations; it creates stagnation, toxicity, and feelings of inadequacy.

This scarcity-based consumer culture that Lynne has identified has most of us living in what she calls an experience of constant deficit, feeling that there's something lacking or something wrong with us which we then try to resolve by obsessively acquiring what we believe we are lacking. Think for a moment how our self-worth has become so entangled in our financial worth. It is a systemic trend that is connected to our value as individuals and organizations.

Sufficiency and fulfillment results from realizing we are enough in who we are. Lynne says, "If I realize that I am enough just the way I am, then I am free to focus on making a difference with my life." She further states, "When we are in touch with our sufficiency, our needs are met."[6]

That solution takes action and the steps to successful execution aren't always immediately clear, but I'm here to help turn a light on pathways to help you see you have the personal power to get you there!

Don't stop with identifying your limiting voices and thoughts. You must also identify the trends connected to them to effectively take action to address them and the damage they do to you. You are enough to disrupt these limiting voices and thoughts. Disrupting them is critical to unleashing the superhero within you and igniting you into action.

Make it happen! You can do it.

Chapter 2 activators

👉 **Reflection questions**:
- ➠ What limiting voices and thoughts can I identify? In what moments are they the loudest and most frequent?
- ➠ How is the trend of a scarcity mindset showing up in my life?

👉 **Personal power tip**: The voice that says you are not enough may never go away. It's okay. Everyday superheroes hear it too. Take its power away by recognizing the trends around when it shows up and quiet and disrupt it in the moment by refocusing your thoughts and energy on what is true.

➠ How do you strike in the moment and create a mindset of I am enough? How do you create a mindset of sufficiency? How do you prevent and disrupt the trends? How do you find a way to move forward when that voice and the limiting thoughts in your head seem to be crippling you? How do you prevent and disrupt that voice and those limiting thoughts that continue even after you've identified that you do have value? Here are some daily, personal power and hope practices that I believe disrupt limiting thoughts, work magic, and ground you in what is true. .

➠ *Prior to the moment:*
1. **Begin and end with gratitude**: Gratitude creates a space of sufficiency and feeling that you are enough. Create a gratitude ritual that works for you. My ritual includes gratitude for things like myself, those who share life and love with me, and the four elements of nature: Earth, fire (sun), water, and air.

2. **Identify manifestation mantras**: Choose and write down manifestation mantras that feel good and say them out loud every day in a quiet space, but particularly the day of that opportunity, that meeting, or that moment. It can be, "I am enough" for example. I say them out loud whether I feel it or not. Just saying them out loud helps shift your mindset and energy, and you can feel it in your body. It may

sound crazy, but it works, and it quiets that voice. It's also been my experience that it helps to reduce the frequency of limiting thoughts and helps me embrace my personal power. For example, I say:

➤ I am enough
➤ I value and believe in myself
➤ I am a powerful light and force
➤ I am a warrior
➤ I am a beautiful goddess
➤ I am a superhero
➤ I am a superstar
➤ I attract and give unconditional love
➤ I attract abundance and prosperity
➤ My personal power creates meaningful impact
➤ I embrace lightness and joy in my life
➤ I bring forth calm and peace
➤ The universe has my back and co-creates with me
➤ The personal power and answers are within me
➤ I stand in a place of hope
➤ Nothing can stop me or purpose

3. **Disrupt the limiting thoughts by using self-talk:** Speak to the limiting thoughts and tell them to leave you. Do it out loud. Disrupt the voice and thoughts before they land. For me, I not only tell them to leave, but I also ask myself, "What is true?" I say it and then reflect on what I know to be true. It helps me remove self-limiting

thoughts and grounds me in what is true, and that I am enough. Follow it with manifestation mantras.

4. **Use visualization**: It is called several things, imagery, visualization, guided meditation. No matter the word used, the concept is the same. It is the creation of a mental image, intention, and process of what you want to happen or feel in reality. See yourself taking the action. See positive results happening. Think about how many times the worst-case scenario pops into your mind. Disrupt it. Flip it to the best-case scenario. I've been using mental imagery since playing sports in my youth and continue to see the positive results from it. The evidence is strong. The impact of positive self-talk, optimism, and mental imagery has been studied for decades by scientists and psychologists. It simply works. That's why Olympians use it. It has been shown to extend life, improve performance, and even reduce anxiety.[7]

5. **Use box breathing**: Breathe in for a count of four, hold for a count of four, and then breathe out for a count of four. Hold for another count of four and then do it again. Do it four times. This is not only a common and effective meditation practice, but also a practice taught to first responders that can bring calm and focus in times of intense anxiety.

➔ *In the moment:*

1. **Breathe**: Take a moment to pause and just breathe deeply. Even if you feel you can't do box breathing in the moment, take just one deep breath. You will immediately feel the difference.

2. **Choose your strongest mantra (or two) and have it ready**: Choose one or two mantras that feel the most powerful to you that can quickly remove limiting thoughts and get you in the right mindset that you are powerful and enough. Use self-talk and speak to yourself and then follow your intuition on next steps.

3. **Use an image that works**: Choose an image that immediately creates a feeling of safety and confidence. I have a friend who imagines Detective Oliva Benson from Law and Order standing beside her. Who is that person or that image that inspires you, creates a feeling of safety for you, reminds you that you are not alone, that you are enough and strong enough to face any challenge?

➤ **Unleash your superhero**: Now that you have researched superheroes, choose one you most connect with. Write down who it is and why you chose them.

➤ **Manifestation affirmation**: Limiting thoughts leave; you have no power over me. I stand in a place of personal power, hope, and what is true.

Be fully and authentically *you* in every moment

Clean out the *shoulds* and expand self-awareness

Once you start to believe that you are enough to create change, disrupt those limiting thoughts. The next step in igniting your personal power is doing your best at showing up authentically in every moment. Easier said than done, right? Well, if you want to become fully who you are, achieve the desires of your heart and make an impactful difference in the world, you have to be authentically you, not just every once in a while, but consistently in every moment.

To do it, you first have to clean out the *shoulds* and develop greater self-awareness. Ask yourself what is true for me? I know I've already briefly talked a little bit about all the *shoulds* that have been present in my life, and all the *shoulds* and expectations that exist for women and historically marginalized groups such as the gender and cultural stereotypes that impact us. These are things that religion, work, society and family tell us we should be. I'm not saying that it's not okay to embrace some of those things but only if it works for you. You have to ask yourself, "Is this really what I want in my life?" "Is this what I fully believe to be true?" I often ask, "Does it feel good, or does it make you nauseous?!" When you think about the *shoulds* in your life, begin to remove the things that you feel don't align with who you are. Yes, I said who you are.

Do you know who you are? Can you even answer that question? When meeting new people, I love to begin the conversation with this prompt: "Tell me who you are, what you value, and a couple stories along your journey that brought you to where and who you are today." Some people get immediately uncomfortable and struggle with finding the words to describe themselves when asked to tell their story. Some use words that were given to them by others. They may even start the response with, "Well, people describe me as…" Still others immediately default to giving me their resume. And then sometimes there are those people who smile because they know the answer, flowing confidently into telling me exactly who they are.

So many of the people who can't confidently flow into answering the question of who they truly are simply haven't taken time to find the answers for themselves. If you have a hard time answering that question, you have some work to do on self-awareness. It's okay. We all do. We are all at different levels of self-awareness and it is a muscle we continue to develop. Your first questions are probably, "Okay, so where do I start?" "How do I discover who I truly am?" "How do I continue to check in with myself?"

Here are some of the lessons I learned and steps I took to develop a healthy self-awareness. Start with the questions, "What is true?" and "What matters most to me?" See where that takes you! Those questions are not only a good place to begin but they are great questions to ground you on a regular basis in what is true for you. I still use them today.

Try doing some personal brand exercises. Asking yourself the questions found in these exercises can help you define what you value as an intrinsic aspect of who you are. One exercise that helped me was the Ikigai framework and exercise. Ikigai is a Japanese concept for that which gives your life worth, meaning, or purpose.[1]

HOW TO FIND IKIGAI

What you love

passion   mission

Your strengths   IKIGAI   The world needs

profession   vocation

What you can be paid for

The Ikigai framework is the convergence of four areas of life: What you love, what you're good at, what the world needs, and what you could be paid for. The very center, where each area overlaps, is your *Ikigai*—your reason for getting up and where to focus your efforts to find fulfillment. Working with a coach and doing exercises like the Ikigai framework, among other exercises, helped me more clearly define my values, my purpose, and my vision. It helped me along my journey of self-awareness.

Another good exercise is writing your eulogy and including one or two things that were instrumental in bringing you to where you are and who you are today. I know it may sound a bit different, but it works. Also, go to somebody that you trust, you feel safe with, and who you believe has a high level of self-awareness and authenticity. They may be the best, outside of yourself, at seeing you for who you are, and they may have identified things that they see in you that sometimes you have had a hard time seeing in yourself that will help you recognize aspects of who you are.

Once you do some initial work, it's important that you establish a regular practice to improve and continue to develop self-awareness. You can't establish a practice of being fully you in every moment and experience fulfillment without self-awareness and continual self-growth. How do you go about creating a practice of becoming more self-aware? There are lots of opinions on that one! It can be overwhelming.

Here is an evidence-based approach that has worked wonders for me.[2] Start with journaling! Your next thought may be where do you start? Well, I had the same question over a decade ago and here is what worked for me. If you have trouble journaling or knowing where to start, begin with a thought journal. Sit down for 15 to 30 minutes and write down ten things that capture your thoughts and attention in your environment. You may find yourself going longer. I like to sit outside and write down what I observe. Write down the details of what is occurring and what is the emotion connected to it. It helps you tune in more closely to your thoughts and emotions. It may be a hummingbird you notice or the wind blowing through the trees. Dig deeper into the emotion and what it may be connected to.

Write in a journal regularly to reflect on your thoughts, connected emotions, and actions. Not only does journaling help with improving self-awareness, but there's mental health benefits to journaling. Numerous studies have shown the benefits to calming anxiety, reducing stress, anxiety, identifying triggers, developing healthy reactions, and more.[3]

What I will also say is what's worked for me is not putting too much structure around it. Journaling can definitely help you with self-reflection, self-awareness, connecting with your emotions, expressing your feelings, trusting your intuition, and it can help you explore and identify vision, purpose, and the desires of your heart while also manifesting them into reality. I envisioned writing this book in September of 2019 and wrote about it in my journal. Four years later on the same day and week in September of 2023, I signed a publishing contract and here I am!

Journaling has truly been a ritual for transformation and manifestation for me, and I love looking back through my journals following my journey of self-awareness and growth. It's also exciting and reassuring to go back and explore some of the emotions and the self-reflection during periods of change in my life, exploring what my intuition was telling me and what manifested when I followed it! Your intuition is rarely wrong, and the universe will have your back. I've seen it. I love the way a friend of mine puts it: "Just give the universe a chance to show you I've got you."

In addition to taking time for reflection and journaling, reflect and journal in spaces that create a feeling of safety and connection. I've found I'm very connected to nature and its surroundings. Nature generates positive emotions for me; it brings peace and calmness and pure joy. It also activates my creative senses. I have a deep respect for the Earth and native wisdom. I have Native American heritage in my family and my great grandmother taught me about animals and their spiritual connectedness. I really enjoy just sitting in nature paying attention to what animals show up. I love looking up the Native American spiritual meanings behind the animal. Many times you will find a deeper meaning behind those occurrences and the messages may encourage, lead to, and activate self-awareness, self-growth, and focused reflection. It may lead to the exact message you need to hear!

Who you are begins and ends with self-awareness and your journey of self-growth. Once you can verbalize who you are and what your values are as easily as saying your name, you can then more effectively and authentically be you in every moment! You can live for yourself and not for others, and not for others' expectations.

Now, I also understand we are not perfect, and that's not the goal. There will be times when we don't show up authentically. That's okay. There is still an opportunity for you to disrupt it even after it has landed. You can show up authentically after the fact by repairing it. Go back to the person or group and admit your lack of authenticity in that previous moment, and then share and show up with your true self and your commitment going forward. You just took that moment back—authentically. Keep working at it. You will get better. You will make mistakes and that's okay. You will also eventually find yourself showing authentically more and more frequently—in every moment.

It's okay to seek information and get help. I started working proactively on my self-awareness and self-growth with a life coach. This helped to accelerate self-growth and helped me find my pathways to successful execution quicker than I could have alone. I didn't stop at the door outside of the closet 19 years ago! I had to continue to learn, grow, and identify for myself who I was and what I wanted to stand for in every moment. I tell people learning the importance of self-awareness work and starting to practice it in my thirties was life changing for me. It helped me develop self-confidence and courage to be fully me. It helped to ignite my personal power. I had to figure out what was true for me and what mattered most without the influence of external factors and all the *shoulds* in my life! It was time to start living for myself.

Live for self not for others

Once you start to fully embrace who you are and begin to live more authentically, you can then start living for you and for self rather than for others and societal expectations. It's important to prioritize self, your wants, and your needs first. That is also being truly authentic in every moment and helps you become a better version of yourself. It's learning to respect yourself. It is true that you cannot respect yourself and you cannot help others unless you're prioritizing and taking care of yourself first. It's called practicing self-love, and it is a lifelong practice.

Women and under-recognized and marginalized groups often find themselves caught up in the *shoulds* and putting a great amount of their energy into pleasing people and living for others. People pleasing is more commonly presented in women than men. Studies have found this behavior is commonly exhibited in the majority of women while only a minority of men show similar tendencies.[4]

Our society places very different expectations on women vs. men. Society has reinforced these "gender roles" or "gender norms." Women are raised to accept social norms that make them susceptible to the dangers of people pleasing. Think about it for a second. Women are often encouraged to be polite, to carefully choose their words when communicating what they want, and to prioritize others' needs over their own. This was not just how my mother was raised, it is the story of many still today. Many gender stereotypes are continuously reinforced in society in a manner that distinctly disadvantages women and non-binary individuals.

Living for others and people pleasing is a common blocker to activating our personal and collective power for change, and it's where many of us find ourselves stuck, unfulfilled, with little forward movement. We find ourselves living for others rather than living for self not only in our personal lives but also in our professional lives. I've struggled with this myself, and I know many others who have as well. Let me tell you about Jun. Her story is all too common.

She worked for a tech company often putting in ten or more hours a day, working well into the evenings and on the weekends. She regularly felt exhausted and said she was always busy. Dedicating her energy to work and family, she was too busy to take care of herself and would routinely sacrifice her self-care time for either family or work. However, she often found it difficult to fully engage with her family or in her work. She felt shame, guilt, and was depressed with life. "I didn't have consistent, healthy practices. I believed I could never get enough work done—there was always more piling up—so I rarely took breaks. And rather than eating healthily every few hours, I would grab food once I was starving, usually making poor choices about what I ate. I also found myself drinking too much alcohol to try to relax in the evenings and then not sleeping enough, only getting four to six hours a night." She continued, "I was monitoring all of my messaging channels throughout the day and into the evening, and I felt the pull to be immediately responsive to all of it. It was exhausting. But I couldn't stop. I craved external validation and needed that to combat the feeling that I was always falling short of the expectations that I believed others had of me and lived in my head," she said.

Very little of her energy was being put into prioritizing herself, but a lot of energy was going into seeking validation and pleasing her colleagues and leaders at work, her family, and others. Jun's self-care practices were inconsistent at best and often non-existent at times, and it was adversely impacting her emotionally, psychologically, and physically. Her body shut down. It took a breakdown and Jun ending up in the hospital to stop what was happening.

Three lifestyle factors form the pillars of good health: diet, exercise, and sleep. Experts call it the wellness triad and when one is off or inadequate, they all are adversely impacted. When these self needs are met, our energy and mood levels, cognitive performance, and immune system operate fully. When they are not met, we experience decreased energy, and an inability to focus and manage our emotional and psychological health. Physically, our bodies begin to deteriorate.

Jun's story is the story of so many others. We live in an always-on culture that expects us to perform and give and perform and give... not to yourself but to others, individuals, and organizations. It took ending up in a hospital bed for Jun to finally rest, renew, and re-evaluate her life. She left with a commitment to live for herself first, to be better for herself, a better version of herself. "It was time for a reset," Jun recalls. What she did next transformed her life.

She began to start her days with meditation and mantras. She set alarms on her watch and phone to build time into her daily schedule for opportunities to breathe and eat. She turned her message notifications off during her break times. She scheduled 20-minute and 50-minute meetings rather than 30 minutes or an hour to prevent back-to-back meetings, affording her time to think, prepare, and be fully present. She actually took lunch and made sure to go outside, even for a short period, twice a day. She used meditation and music to manage her stress in the evenings rather than alcohol. She started getting more regular exercise and eight hours of sleep at night.

"I really forced myself to create space and time so that I could rest, renew, and reflect, and I made it a priority to do things for myself throughout my day, even if only a few minutes each time," she told me. She worked to remove the self-limiting thoughts that she was just too busy and didn't have time to give to herself and instead she started telling herself what was true. What was true was that she was prioritizing work and others over herself.

She started some of the self-awareness and meditation practices I have already mentioned in the previous chapters. She began to devote time to herself first and to what mattered most to her. She had had a good idea of what her values were and had even spoken about those values to others, but she was not living them authentically herself. Taking those steps resulted in her performance actually improving and her energy levels increasing. Giving time to her passions and what breaks her heart renewed her purpose in life. By giving to herself first, it actually improved the experiences and time she gave to her family and her work. Her overall health and

well-being as well as her level of personal happiness and fulfillment also greatly improved.

So many people are living life non-stop at a ferocious
pace in pursuit of pleasing and living for others. They rarely
stop to ask themselves who they are, what is true, what they
stand for, and what matters most to them. They rarely stop
for personal renewal and rest. They rarely ask for help.

So many people are stuck and live in a state of exhaustion
trying to meet the *shoulds* that live in their minds and the
expectations of others. It drives their focus and actions down
a path of destruction. If this sounds familiar, the good news
is you can always disrupt that path even after it has already
landed no matter how long you have been on it. It's time to
live for self rather than for others. You cultivate your authenticity and personal power when you create time and space to
love and prioritize yourself. In giving to yourself first, you can
unleash your superhero power to then give to others and to
the world.

Focus on "being"

We can often get caught in the erroneous belief that the
more we do the more value we have. We believe it's the way
to achieve the desires of our heart while also creating positive
change, resulting in joy and fulfillment in our lives. If doing
is your practice, I'm willing to bet you find yourself feeling
exhausted and unfulfilled. I'm going to tell you to consider
shifting from a practice of focusing on doing all you think
you should all the time to being who you are.

It's very difficult to eliminate the *shoulds*, step fully into
who you are, and continually grow in self-awareness and prioritize self, when your focus is primarily doing. It strips and
takes away your energy to activate your personal power. I'm
going to tell you to shift your focus and energy to being. Yes,
you heard me right. I'm asking you to focus more on being

rather than doing and allow the universe to help co-create with you. I am not saying do nothing, just don't allow the focus of doing to become your first priority. I'm saying stop trying to control everything, focus on being, and the doing will become more clear to you and aligned with who you are.

Focus on also being open to experiences however they show up. Embark on the next journey and adventure that calls you. Step out of your comfort zone. Don't try to fit into any label or control it. Just be you and embrace the new paths, opportunities, and possibilities that will unfold before you, calling you to action. Sometimes when we're focused too much on doing rather than being, we miss what the universe might have offered up as an opportunity or pathway more aligned with our purpose and who we truly are.

Be open and find joy and growth in experiences. Believe in the magic of experiences. Some may last a moment, and some may last a lifetime. It is in those experiences that you find that you grow and that you find who you are. Go after and begin to manifest the experiences you want, and that you feel you fit within—the uniqueness that is you that no label can fully encompass. Embrace who you are unconditionally and authentically. Embrace what feels right for you.

It is a waste of your energy and damaging to self-growth and awareness to attempt to fit within a label or a puzzle piece or an expectation that society and others created for you. Just being who you are is enough. It is powerful. It can not only bring healing for you, but it can bring healing for others. It ignites your personal power and inspires others to take action.

Stop focusing so much first and foremost on doing and just be and see what comes to you—what magic occurs. Know that the universe has put you in this place at this time for a purpose and the universe will not abandon you when you need help. It will co-create with you. Disrupt the limiting thoughts and let the universe remind you that you alone have everything it takes within you to be fully who you are and achieve your dreams.

Sometimes we need to stop trying to control and author every detail of our lives and allow the universe to co-create with us what is next. Just be you. You have nothing to prove. Be mindful in every moment. Show up. Keep showing up. Showing up is just being you in every moment. That is an act of respecting yourself and loving yourself. Just remember you are not alone and there is power in just being—being who you are and sharing that with the world.

There's nothing wrong with planning but resist the pull to control, to create a particular form, to fix it, and to go into a hypervigilant state daily. Don't over index on trying to control it, shape it, and do! Find the courage to allow what's next to take shape and co-create it with the universe. Push away fear and become comfortable with the unknown.

Sit alone, create time and space for yourself to just be you and pay attention, listen, and observe what you are hearing in those moments—those moments when you're not doing and you're just being. The next pathway to purpose, passion, and unleashing your superhero powers may appear. The building blocks and next pathway to self-awareness and self-growth may appear. The pathway to your vision and the manifestation of your hopes and dreams beyond what you can imagine may come to life. Create space and time to just be all that makes you YOU and for the universe to do its magic.

Have a practice of removing wrong perceptions and expectations that do not serve you. Have a practice of being you. Rise up to be you and make it happen! I'm going to tell you that just being fully you has purpose and power in it, not only for yourself but for others. Showing up fully—fully embracing who you are and sharing that with others in every moment—will activate personal and collective power for both individual and social change. Who you are is uniquely powerful and positive change and movement can happen when you rise up fully in who you are in every moment.

Chapter 3 activators

⟆ Reflection questions:

➤ What *shoulds* and expectations are present in my life that have impacted or continue to impact my choices and who I am? Is this really what I want in my life? Is this what I fully believe to be true? When I think about the expectations and *shoulds* in my life, what does not align with what I believe to be my true self?

➤ How much energy and prioritization do I put into focusing on doing compared to just being who I am?

⟆ Personal power tip: It's time to ignite your personal power with journaling! Take time to stop, reflect, and journal regularly. Put it on the calendar but also do it in moments when ideas or messages begin to show up for you. Journaling can definitely help you with self-reflection, self-awareness, connecting with your emotions, expressing your feelings, trusting your intuition, and it can help you explore and identify vision, purpose, and the desires of your heart while also manifesting them into reality. Journaling can become for you a ritual for transformation and manifestation. Document your journey—this will show you from where you have come and provide clarity on where you are going, which will help ignite your personal power over and over again.

⟆ Unleash your superhero: Now that you have chosen your superhero you most connect with, choose a favorite quote from your superhero. Write down that favorite quote from them and reflect on it. A quote that inspires and encourages you. Write down the thoughts that come to you.

🔥 **Manifestation affirmation**: There is power, purpose, and magic in being me and sharing it with the world. The universe has my back. I have everything I need within me to achieve the desires of my heart.

Find purpose and pathways in what breaks your heart

It begins with one person—one match-strike. That person is you

Stop right now. Stop reading for a moment. Yes, that's what I said. Put this book down. You've created time and space to read it and now I want you to create space to reflect for 5 to 10 minutes. Ask yourself, "What is breaking my heart?" "What have I observed in my personal life and my professional life or in the world around me that often comes to me in my thoughts, that keeps capturing my attention?" Maybe it's a current personal experience or an experience of a colleague or harm happening in your community. Hold on to it and we'll come back to it.

Even though you've experienced rejection, you recognize you have value. Even though the voice that tells you you are not enough may never go away, you recognize and work at embracing your personal power and using practices to disrupt the limiting thoughts. You begin understanding your trends and working on the most effective approach that ignites your personal power.

Now it is time to recognize and embrace that you, one person, in being fully and authentically who you are, can achieve the desires of your heart, and you can make an impactful difference in your life and in the world. You must believe that you as one person can make a difference even if you're the only one in the room who's feeling a heart calling you to action.

Believing is powerful. Believing is key to manifesting. I remember my father always told me just keep believing in yourself and when you feel like not believing find a way to rise up and believe again. I have the word believe tattooed on my right wrist over a star. My father would always take time to remind me I was a superstar. He would point to the stars in the sky and tell me don't you ever forget you are a star. Every one of those stars up there is a beautiful, unique, and powerful light. You're one of those stars and never stop believing that. Never stop believing that just one star can bring light to the sky. My father called me a superstar so many times that I would roll my eyes at him as a teen. As an adult, it became one of my favorite manifestation mantras that brings me courage and hope and helps move me to action.

I don't know how many times people have reached out to me and asked me how I achieved leadership and mission-driven success, for example, in places like Uber, or how I became so courageous, confident, and successful at execution. How did I move an organization or leader from a "no" to a "yes," from a fearful and hesitant place to a creative, resourceful, and confident space? How did I rally others to join me? It began with me valuing and believing in myself, relentlessly believing that I, as one person, could make a difference, and manifesting what I believed while also empowering others to do the same.

I've heard it in the past over and over again, and I continue to hear it today. People ask me for help and then as I hear more about their reluctance to take action, I hear similar things like, "Can I really make a difference if I'm not an expert?" "I don't know that I really have a story that's powerful enough to create change?" "I'm sure there are other people that are better able to address this." "It's too big." "I'm fearful of how people will respond." "How can I create change at my age?" I hear them talk about moments of opportunity, but often they come with self-doubt and statements that are self-limiting.

People struggle with believing in the personal power in who they are as an individual, and how their individual power and actions can help ignite more action. Courage fuels confidence and confidence is contagious. When your heart and intuition are calling you, they are calling you for a reason. So many people feel intuitively that pull to act on behalf of themselves or others and just ignore it and walk away.

Don't ignore what is breaking your heart. Don't ignore your intuition. Don't ignore what is causing discomfort and maybe anger to rise up in you. There is purpose there. Often, the desires of your heart, pathways to your personal power, and opportunities to make a difference can be found in what is breaking your heart. Don't wait on something or someone else.

Don't you think maybe the reason you are feeling the repetitive tugging at your heart to act is because you are able to do exactly what you are being drawn to do? The truth is you are the one who is able and appropriately positioned where you are to make an impactful difference in your own life and the lives of others. Your actions can be the match-strike needed to ignite others to similar, courageous action.

When people are able to recognize and embrace their own value and their personal power, they are then able to move into action believing they can make a difference. The superhero within them gets unleashed. Let me remind you that perfection is not the end goal. It is a continuous journey of self-growth and acceptance, battling those limiting thoughts and voices of self-doubt. But we do become stronger, and it becomes less difficult.

There are a lot of what you might call "everyday people" making their way through life who then experience or observe rejection and harm along their journey. This might be harm to another human being, harm to humanity, harm to the Earth, or harm to themselves. It captures their attention, and they start to feel the currents of their heart drawing them to take action. Many times it must start with that individual action and the individual belief and choice to take action that is a catalyst for other individual and collective action.

I know people who have chosen to stop and act, rather than walk away; they step in while battling those limiting thoughts in order to create meaningful change. One of those people is Dr. Topeka Sam.

While attending college in Baltimore, Topeka dated a man who sold drugs. Even though she never used the drugs, she became caught up in the lifestyle and what the drug money offered her, becoming a broker between people looking to buy the drugs and those selling.

Her experience with drugs resulted in an arrest and indictment in Virginia many years later after a federal drug sting operation. Facing up to 20 years in prison, she explained that she pleaded guilty "and became part of a new community in prison."

She spent over 20 hours a day in her isolation cell, so she took classes to create an opportunity to engage with others. "When I heard the stories of so many women and the impact incarceration had on them, not only did I recognize the adverse impact of drugs on these women, their families, and communities, but I found that there were almost always similar underlying issues," Topeka said.

Instead of the issues you might expect to see on the surface impacting women, like being poor, White, Black, and coming from low socio-economic backgrounds with little to no education, she found that women in federal prison were doctors, lawyers, senators, and judges. And in story after story, these women shared similar stories of childhood trauma, sexual and domestic violence, mental health issues, and substance abuse issues.

"I knew that when I left prison, I could do anything that I wanted to do because of the support system I had in place before prison. However, that was not the story for so many others that I met," Topeka told me. Many of these women would have very little to no support upon release back into society. One day, she felt the currents of heart compelling her to take action. So she listened—and did something she had never done before. She made a decision to start up a non-profit organization called The Ladies of Hope Ministries (LOHM), an organization whose mission is to help disenfranchised and marginalized women transition back into society after incarceration through providing education, supporting entrepreneurship, focusing on spiritual empowerment, and advocacy for all women impacted by the criminal justice and prison system.

Her vision became a reality in 2015 after receiving a reduced sentence. While in prison, she witnessed firsthand the epidemic and disparity of incarceration on women, more specifically women of color. She felt the urgency to bring the faces and voices of women in prison to the public in order to bring awareness to women's incarceration and post-incarceration issues in an attempt to change the criminal justice and legal system.

Today, Topeka manages several full-time employees and The LOHM has raised over $10 million dollars. She works with contractors and consultants and supports thousands of women and girls worldwide. She's worked with national corporations like Chanel, Google, the NFL, and many others driving change. She's built housing units in New York, New Orleans, and Maryland. Additionally, the organization has reconnected families and secured job opportunities for those receiving support.

Now Topeka will tell you she doesn't do any of this alone. Many people have joined her in her mission and her vision. Her individual actions ignited and empowered others to do the same work and to believe in the same mission and vision. It took her, as an individual person, to choose not to walk away from the harm she experienced herself and witnessed in countless others. Topeka created a movement from what angered her and broke her heart.

You can too. It starts with one person and that one person is you. You are enough. Listen. Look closely to find the pathways to ignite your personal power and purpose in what is breaking your heart to enable change to happen.

Make time to stop, listen, and reflect

There have been many books written on purpose. I spent a long period of my life reading those books, looking for purpose. I couldn't always communicate my purpose. If somebody asked me what my purpose or vision was, I didn't know what to say. I hoped they would not ask me that question. I didn't know exactly how to answer it. I looked for it. I chased it. I pursued finding purpose, ultimately without success. People make lots of money trying to help people find their purpose in their lives. Much of it is a waste of money and time.

You don't have to read a bunch of books, or seek a ton of advice, although it can be helpful depending on the source. But you probably won't find your purpose in a book. You most likely won't find it in a system or institution that tells you what it thinks your purpose should be. I believe you find purpose from within, in who you are and often in what is breaking your heart, and pathways that create opportunities for making a difference can be found there. Let me tell you how I found my purpose, how I continue to find it, and how I believe you can find it.

Let's get back to that 5 or 10 minutes when I asked you to stop. It took stopping, listening, and reflecting for me to find it. One of the most important ways to find purpose and to keep yourself grounded in what is true is to STOP in your busy day to day and your drive for doing more and take some time to practice reflection. You have to stop. You have to give yourself permission. You have to give yourself permission to stop and take time to listen and reflect.

So what does that look like? It looks like this: Separate yourself from your normal day-to-day activities for a period of time. Distract your mind so that it's not racing and focused on doing and all the other things going on in your life. You have to be able to sit in silence or else you won't hear your soul and heart speak in all the noise around you. When I say silence, that doesn't always mean complete silence. It's silence from the typical noise in your daily life. Sitting with sounds of nature or calming music may also get you into the right state of mind.

When you're caught up in the daily noise and doing, listening to the voice that tells you that you're too busy to stop, you can't hear or see what your soul, heart, and the universe may want you to see and hear in what is breaking your heart. It makes it difficult to hear, and it's easy to dismiss or miss important details and messages the universe may have for you.

When you sit in silence, thoughts, creative ideas, purpose, and pathways will begin to appear and come to you. You have to create a space where you can stay in the moment and be present, feel your emotions and listen to your intuition, noticing the subtle signs you would otherwise miss or ignore. I love Albert Einstein's quote: "I think 99 times and find nothing. I stop thinking, swim in silence, and truth comes to me."

Now I get it is easier said than done. Creating space and time to stop and swim in silence was always very difficult for me because my mind was always active and focused on doing. I'm always on the move, and I have intense energy. Maybe you can relate. I always convinced myself I was too busy, and I didn't have enough time. Remember that scarcity mindset I wrote about. I knew that well. It was a close friend of mine. It still is at times.

I would have a hard time stopping long enough to quiet my mind, listen, and reflect. I wouldn't take time to really disconnect. The reality was it was also very difficult for me to find ways that I could distract my mind. I couldn't stop the thoughts from racing. I tried the typical practices like meditation, but the recommendations didn't always work for me.

I finally had to create my own practice, which became my way of doing everything! I had to disrupt the limiting beliefs and find a combination of things that worked and felt right for me to be successful at it. It would ultimately help lead me to finding much more than purpose and pathways to making a difference in what broke my heart. It also reinvigorated me, gave me rest, led to vision, brought manifestations to life, accelerated self-growth, and helped me identify opportunities to unleash my superhero personal power!

Here are some things that have worked for me that may work for you:

1. **Try to make it a daily practice but be flexible and kind with yourself and set yourself up for success**. I started with an uninterrupted 5 minutes, then I went to 15 minutes and then 30 minutes. Sometimes I even do an hour, but I also sometimes miss days.
2. **Choose the best time of day**. Choose the time of day that is your most creative, most open, and is the least likely time that you will be distracted. For me, that is the morning. I treat it like exercise and put it on my schedule and keep it routine, which helps me stay accountable to myself. Set boundaries with family, friends, and colleagues to respect that time and space.
3. **Begin with a distraction**. Find something that completely distracts you from the typical noise and what may be currently racing in your mind from family, work responsibilities, and daily "to dos." Use the first 5 to 10 minutes to distract your mind. It could be a smell, a breathing exercise, a short walk, something visual, gardening, watching birds outdoors, playing with an animal.

4. **Choose a location that supports the first three suggestions above and helps to draw in the right energy to focus and ground you.** For me, it is outside in nature or in a space (small or large) that I can dedicate and create an environment that supports meditation and reflection time.
5. **Ground yourself in what is true and incorporate the personal power and hope practices.** This will help you daily stay grounded in what is true and feels purposeful to you.
6. **Find what works for you!** Experiment with all of the above and more and find what works for you. You will find it!

Life happens and you will miss a day here and there. But don't go days without feeding and resting your soul and creating time to stop, listen, and reflect. Put the brakes on if you go a week without it. I believe it's also critically important to try to make and pick out times during the month where you can give yourself two to three hours to reflect. You'll find that this will really breathe life and purpose into you.

One of the practices that my best friend invited me into years ago was new and full moon rituals. I've maintained it, and it helps keep me accountable to myself. We put it on the calendar every new moon and full moon that occurs every month. We also hold one another accountable and also invite others to join us. I take time that morning or evening to stop, listen, and reflect for an hour or two. I also read about the Native American and astrological meanings of the specific timing, which often opens the door to additional reflection, release, and opportunities for manifestation as well as messages that resonate with me providing encouragement and affirmation.

It's also a great time to come together collectively with others, share reflections and manifestations, and encourage one another. It creates space for support, connection, and collective action. It's a time to breathe in purpose and time to manifest dreams and desires. It's time for shared gratitude and time to honor the Earth and all it provides us. It truly helps me stop, reflect, prioritize self, and focus on what matters most in life while also connecting with others.

These practices help me reset and restart if needed. It also brings with it accountability with people who have shared energy and who genuinely care and love me, and I for them. It is in those times when I take more time to reflect whether a couple hours, a half a day, or multiple days, that some of my greatest ideas, manifestations, visions, and pathways to using my personal power to make a difference have come to me.

If you really want to challenge yourself, take three to four days every quarter and go to a location and stop, listen, and reflect. It's been life changing for me. It is where I have connected with the currents of my heart and found direction and clarity. It has breathed life into me. It was in one of those times that this book and its message came to me!

When you gift yourself time and space and connect with yourself, you will feel your intuition and where the currents of your heart are drawing you. During that time, pay attention to where your heart is leading you and what is capturing your attention. Where is it telling you to step up? What is yourself speaking to you about? What is the universe revealing to you in your experiences or surroundings? They have a message you need to hear. Write down what you're hearing and thinking. It will come to you.

Stop and reflect on what is breaking your heart. Feel the currents. It's in those currents you will find purpose and pathways where your personal power can be ignited, unleashing the superhero within you.

There will be repetitive signs

What keeps showing up is asking you to show up. Have you ever heard the saying that if you slow down, things will speed up? Ideas, thoughts, and hunches will come to you. When you choose to slow down, stop, listen, and reflect, think about what those thoughts are, messages or signs that have been appearing on a regular basis to you—repetitively.

What are those thoughts, ideas, or signs that keep being brought to your conscious mind? Maybe a connection or colleague has reappeared who might be connected in some way to where your heart is drawing you. Maybe it's a news article that you just ran across connected to that thing that's breaking your heart. Maybe you just got invited to an event with a friend. Maybe a grasshopper landed on or near you more than once as you thought about what was breaking your heart. Yes, I said a grasshopper. Look up the spiritual meaning of that one!

Are you moving too fast to notice? Have you shrugged off, dismissed something that may seem subtle at first? If something (a person, animal, place, idea, thing) keeps finding its way to you, into your path, your head, your experiences, and if it's happening repeatedly, purpose is calling you to unleash your superhero.

Let me tell you what it might also show up with. They are those limiting thoughts. You might also hear a voice telling you: "I'm not an expert, what can I really do?" "I don't feel like I can do anything to change my circumstances." "I'm just one person." "Will anybody value my input or actions?" "Am I enough?" "Will my circumstances get better?"

The limiting thoughts will appear along with what might also be breaking your heart. Pay close attention. When purpose is calling, it keeps finding you. There will be repetitive signs, coincidences, and serendipitous moments. Take notice of those things that capture your attention. In them there may be a deeper meaning and a deeper purpose behind it. If it keeps showing up, it's calling you to show up—with a cape on!

As a police officer, I found purpose and pathways in what broke my heart. I found purpose watching how first responders had failed at responding to reports of harm to women and other marginalized groups. One of the spaces that broke my heart was watching how victims/survivors of sexual assault were treated when they reported their assaults to police.

They were often not believed and not taken seriously. The reports were often mishandled and not given the same attention and care as other types of reports. I would many times use this example: Think about how police respond when your house has been broken into. You call them. They respond starting from a position and place of belief. They immediately respond. They show up and they gather evidence. They treat you as if what you're reporting actually happened. That's a property crime. Don't you think they should take crimes against humans, like rape, much more seriously? That's not often the case with harm like sexual violence. When someone reports a sexual assault, most often a woman or non-binary individual, the initial response of many first responders often comes from space of disbelief, influenced by gender and cultural stereotypes along with a lack of knowledge and understanding of the impact of trauma. And it's not just first responders. Those are common beliefs and responses that are prevalent across the world.

The questions and attitudes come from a place of "What did you do to cause this?" I saw firsthand how victims and survivors were disregarded and their stories and reports dismissed and not believed by first responders. That was just the beginning. Not only did I witness the treatment myself, but stories kept finding their way to me. As a police officer, I saw all kinds of harm. The stories of harm were endless. I saw nearly everything that could happen to a human being, but it was something about sexual assault and the treatment of survivors that kept finding its way to me.

It broke my heart, and it called me to do more. But my limiting thoughts tried to convince me otherwise. I absolutely questioned myself, asking "What could I really do?"

The problem was so great. Who would listen to me? I wondered. I didn't really have time to go after trying to fix this big problem when there was so many more to fix in policing. Would the culture ever change? I saw one woman after another being treated in a way they did not deserve. And it wasn't just my department. It was a systemic problem that seemed way too large to tackle.

The limiting thoughts were stopping me from taking action, but they weren't stopping my heart from aching. I didn't know it at the time, but my heart was calling me to purpose—to make a difference where I was at. There were repetitive events, repetitive messages, and repetitive people connected to this issue that kept showing up in my path. It was calling me to show up. Rather than continue to push it away, I began to disrupt and push the limiting thoughts away, and I chose to show up. I found purpose in what was breaking my heart and ignited my personal power and took action.

I started creating time and space to learn more and engage more in the space of sexual assault prevention and response. I gathered and assembled anyone who would help and join me: Advocates, fellow officers, and survivors. They showed up. I led the collaboration and creation of educational initiatives, trainings, and awareness campaigns to help improve the way my department responded to reports of sexual assault.

The training I led became certified training, and before long, my team and I were training multitudes of officers and it expanded to others like court and emergency personnel. I recall one of the training sessions we did for my department. As part of the training, survivors volunteered to share their story in its entirety to help police officers understand the totality of the impact on their lives. I invited one woman to participate who I knew would connect with the group. She had her own personal connection to policing that she shared, coming from a law enforcement family. She had experienced both the best and worst from police interactions along her journey. She began her story from a place of empathy and care, which opened a space for her to be heard and seen by others rather than dismissed.

It was through hers and many other survivors sharing the entirety of their experience that we witnessed the power in human connection and personal stories. I would watch people walk into those rooms with their arms crossed, on their phones, sitting in the back of the room, grumbling, "Here we go with another training telling us something that we do wrong." But as the survivors shared their impactful experiences, we saw that attitude shift quickly. We witnessed some of the hardest hearts melt before our eyes. It was the result of the power and courage of those women who walked in there, stood tall, and told their stories of harm by people, and many times by those people who were responsible for protecting us.

I remember how incredible it was to see the energy and attention change so quickly in the room. I saw the shift from a room full of closed minds and hearts to a room full of heavy hearts and tears. The training literally transformed the way many of those officers viewed sexual assault and impacted how they would respond to reports in the future. It certainly didn't change everyone, but the training and the stories unexpectedly reached some of the toughest to reach. I recall one officer in particular, who we will call Steve. My experience with him, along with many others, was that he was one of the biggest assholes to work with. He was always very vocal about how he felt about the issue of sexual assault and women and his opinions were ugly. I could be much more descriptive, but let's just say he was not kind and respectful. I couldn't stand to be near him.

After the training concluded, I was taken aback when Steve came up to me and thanked me, the advocates, and the survivors. Speaking directly to the survivors, he said, "I feel terrible about how I've treated people in the past who have suffered the kinds of abuse you have suffered and been brave enough to report it." With tears in his eyes, he continued, "I want to apologize to all of you." He told us that, while it was no excuse, he just didn't fully understand the issue and the full impact, and he had appreciated everyone taking the time to educate someone like him. My dislike for him quickly turned to compassion as I witnessed a genuine moment that changed someone's life and would undoubtedly go forward to change the lives of many others.

I had felt that Steve was unreachable, not worth my time. Witnessing this change in him impacted me greatly in how I would look at people like him moving forward. It made me realize that deciding to do something about what was breaking my heart gave not only me a platform but also gave a platform to other people to use their voice and their stories to change lives. Those moments would not have happened had I not followed the currents of where my heart was calling me.

I was reminded that my actions alone, my personal power, could help drive change and inspire and empower others to do the same. The universe didn't stop there and neither did I. Those actions opened the door to more opportunities to make a difference, speaking on conference stages to help raise awareness and empower others, and speaking to various groups and organizations to collaborate on solutions and the co-creation of innovative campaigns and initiatives.

Those actions I took also eventually caught attention and took me to Uber corporate in San Francisco, a much bigger platform and community to create tech solutions and programs that could reach and impact millions of people, including initiatives to prevent sexual misconduct and violence. As the Head of Women's Safety and Gender-Based Violence, I focused on overall safety technology and safety and inclusion programs but had a specific focus on the safety of women and marginalized groups. Another pathway and opportunity had appeared for igniting my personal power for purpose, investing in and assembling others, and making a difference in the world in what broke my heart. Uber would never have become a reality for me if I had not given what was breaking my heart space to manifest. I followed it and it expanded into more opportunities.

You don't have to go searching for purpose. Many people are on a quest to find purpose in their lives. It's not in some place that's unknown to you. It might be in your home, in your community, or in your workplace. It is within you. You don't have to look that hard. You can find it right where you're at. It's been my experience that the universe reveals purpose for us in the moments and in the spaces we're engaging in. It waits for you. It calls you. Stop and listen. Your actions create space for others to hear and act.

We can make a difference with the skills, abilities, and personal power we have in who we are. But first we have to stop, slow down, and pay attention or we will miss it. I'm sure you're starting to notice there's a theme here. Stop, listen, and reflect. Pay attention and the pathway to purpose will start to reveal itself.

Take time to ask yourself what is happening around me, in my home, in my community, in my workplace that is capturing my heart and attention. Maybe it's a pretty big, systemic problem that impacts the world, but it happens to show up in your home, in your workplace, in your community. You can do something to positively impact it right where you're at. The spaces you are in, the experiences, the engagements you have each and every day can provide you with small and big moments to make a difference in your own personal life and the lives of others.

I promise you that activating your personal power can deeply impact and chip away at the bigger problem, and you never know when doing something right within your community may open the door and expand into something much, much bigger with impact beyond what you can imagine. That happened to me, it's happened to many others, and it can happen for you.

It also doesn't always have to be some big initiative in your mind. Maybe you directly change one person's heart and in changing that one person it positively impacts others. When you take that action and make that decision to use your personal power to do something about what is breaking your heart, particularly when it comes from a place of genuine care and integrity, the universe will often reveal opportunities for you to have another conversation and inspire another heart. There is purpose right now in what is breaking your heart.

Are you listening? Self and what's showing up in your surroundings has a message you need to hear. Spend time alone and feel the currents of your heart and where you are being drawn. Take notice of the things that capture your attention and curiosity for it is in these that a much deeper awareness and purpose can arise creating pathways and opportunities to unleash the superhero within you.

Chapter 4 activators

🕯 **Reflection questions**:

➤ Ask yourself again. What is breaking my heart? What have I observed in my personal life and my professional life or in the world that often comes to me in my thoughts, that keeps grabbing my attention?

➤ How am I being drawn to act on what is breaking my heart? What do I really want to do? What is stopping me from taking the action I am drawn to take about what is breaking my heart?

🕯 **Personal power tip**: Create space and time to stop, listen, and reflect daily. Start with 5, 10, or 15 minutes. Once you get into the flow, you will find yourself going longer. If this is already your practice, challenge yourself to also do an entire day or multiple days a quarter. One practice that really helps me make my reflection time more effective is to dedicate time before I dive into reflection to finding something to distract and disrupt the noise and thoughts racing through my head. To prepare for short periods of reflection time, going outside in nature or even my backyard does this for me. For longer reflection periods, from one day to multiple days in a row, I often go to an antique shop! Yes, I said I go to an antique shop (smiling). I go where there are multiple forms of external stimuli that quickly distract my mind from the limiting thoughts and everyday noise and "to dos." It creates a clearing where I can then set my intention and get into a flow for reflection for those longer periods of time. It may sound crazy, but it is quite effective for me. Find what works for you and make it happen!

◊ **Unleash your superhero**: Share the superhero you chose, the superhero you most connect with, and share it with a trusted, close friend and/or chosen family member. Tell them who it is, your favorite quote by them, and why you relate and connect to that specific superhero. Ask them what superhero character they most connect with.

◊ **Manifestation affirmation**: I have personal power in who I am to create meaningful impact in what breaks my heart. I choose to stop, listen, reflect, and follow where the currents of my heart are drawing me. Ideas, purpose, and opportunities for action are flowing to me and pathways are being revealed.

Use your most powerful tool: Your voice

Share what's breaking your heart

Your voice is your most powerful tool. It's a superhero tool. You have the opportunity to show up as your best, true self through your voice. A voice that is authentic and speaks truth from a place of integrity can create impactful change for yourself and others. It can lift people up and ignite action.

Using your voice to share your personal story and the message of your heart—what is breaking your heart—is one of the most powerful ways to use your superhero tool. I shared earlier that it will come to you. You can find purpose and pathways in what breaks your heart. It is often found right where you are. It can also be found in your own personal story. There is tremendous personal power in your story. It can empower and create safety for others. It can create an impactful difference beyond what you can imagine.

With silence, nothing changes. I love Meghan Markle's quote about remaining silent that she provided while giving a speech to Immaculate Heart High School. She said she was initially nervous about speaking out on George Floyd's death. She came to recognize it was not a time for silence. "I wasn't sure what I could say to you," she said to the students. "I wanted to say the right thing and I was really nervous that it would get picked apart. And I realized the only wrong thing to say is to say nothing."[1]

There are those limiting thoughts again. Those limiting thoughts of self-doubt often silence our voices. We worry how it will be received. We question its impact. Using our voices effects change and builds community through empowering others. I agree with Meghan. The only wrong thing to say is to say nothing.

Meghan has been an activist using her voice since she was young. At 11 years old, she saw a commercial for Ivory Soap that depicted women in cultural stereotypes like washing dishes is the duty of women. Rather than remaining silent, Meghan took a stand and took action, writing a letter to Procter & Gamble asking them to change the commercial and use more inclusive language in it. She asked them to change it to "people all over America are fighting greasy pots and pans"—not just women. They changed the commercial, and Meghan realized at an early age the impact she could have with her voice.

Meghan also recently broke her silence around her personal experiences—her personal story, including her experiences as a member of the royal family, being a woman of color, and her pregnancy loss. It was not easy, and it took tremendous courage, but she has positively influenced millions as a result.

Sharing personal stories takes bravery. They are deeply personal and may be difficult to share, but they have the power to drive connection and change. Sometimes you'll find purpose in your own personal story when sharing it. In fact, stories of personal experience are some of the most powerful and purposeful. That includes your own lived experience as well as the stories of others. It truly brings a human component and opportunity to change hearts. It creates space for others to feel safe and supported, particularly women, the LGBTQ+ community, and other marginalized groups.

It requires vulnerability and strength. It creates a space for yourself as well as others to know they are not alone. Stepping into a space of vulnerability and sharing inspires, elevates, and encourages others to embrace a shared vision and purpose. It creates space for us, all of us, to be seen and heard. Being vulnerable and sharing your story can bring meaning and purpose into your life but it also creates belonging, empathy, and understanding, helping shift perspectives and inspire collective action. It helps drive change through human connection.

A growing body of research shows that the need to connect socially with others is as basic as our need for food, water, and shelter, according to Matthew Lieberman who is a professor of biobehavioral science at UCLA's Semel Institute for Neuroscience and Human Behavior. Human connection is also instrumental in changing minds.[2]

You can create that human connection with your personal story. Weaving your personal story into your interactions with others can generate that spark that is needed to create movement. As a leader at Uber, I worked with global teams across the world creating opportunities to meet with expert non-governmental organizations (NGOs) focused on supporting women, the LGBTQ+ community, and all people of color.

I, along with other superheroes, helped bring these groups in the community into Uber, building connections and partnerships with the teams on the inside, creating opportunities to work in collaboration, and developing education and initiatives that focused on safety and inclusion of historically marginalized communities.

I frequently traveled to our international offices to meet personally with teams and identify groups within their own communities. The teams deeply appreciated it. One year I made my way to France to meet with the French Uber team. I loved my French team, and I was excited about spending time in person with them. They were excited too. It was a powerful, beautiful visit. When the French team found out that I was coming, they set up several meetings with media and regulators, including a meeting and visit to the office of the Minister of Gender Equality. We scheduled meetings with several women's feminists' groups since the team's priority focus was women's safety. However, I always strongly encouraged teams to include groups supporting the LGBTQ+ community. It took a little work convincing them of its shared importance, and eventually I got the team to add a relevant group to our meetings.

Teams in the international offices were always very kind and generous with my time. They wouldn't ask for much because we had a lot to accomplish in a small amount of time during my visit, usually only a few days to a week. But I loved the time with them, hearing their unique perspectives, learning about them personally, learning about their country, and the cultural nuances of the region. I believed it was very important to understand and address the specific needs of their region.

The French team was excited to schedule time for me to speak to the French Women of Uber ERG (employee resource group) while in France. They asked me to speak on women's safety. The day before the meeting, one woman who worked in the Uber office on the French team, but was not otherwise involved in my visit, sought me out and caught me in the hallway. I had never met her before. I could tell she was a little anxious and apologetic for stopping me in the hallway. "I couldn't find any time on your calendar," she said, "and I desperately need to speak with you." I promptly delayed my next meeting and created time to speak with her.

She told me that she led the Uber Pride ERG group in France focused on the LGBTQ+ community. She said she was an ally who deeply cared about the community. She shared with me the state of violence facing the LGBTQ+ community in France. I would soon learn even more from a regional LGBTQ+ NGO. In the region, there had been about a 40% increase in violence and harm that year against the LGBTQ+ community.

She told me about how much she cared for the community with tears forming in her eyes. "I am one of only a few others leading and working with the Uber Pride group in France," she said. "We're struggling to get other employees involved, to join and get active in the group and the community. I feel like I've tried everything to get more people involved and nothing is working." She was distraught and she was coming to me for help. She knew I was a Queer woman and leader within the company, that I had been very vocal about being a member of the LGBTQ+ community, and that I was on the leadership committee for the Uber Pride corporate ERG at Uber's global headquarters in San Francisco. In her mind, I had the best shot at getting people's attention to do more.

My heart went out to her. Here she was a cisgender, straight woman who was trying to make a difference for people like me. It made sense now why it had been difficult for me to initially get the teams involved in equally giving attention to groups in the LGBTQ+ community. It was not that they didn't care but their priority focus was on getting more attention and support for women's safety, an equally important initiative. I hugged and thanked her and made sure she knew how people like me greatly valued the actions people like her were taking on our behalf. I told her I would find a way to help her.

When I walked into a large space filled with only women for my talk to the Women of Uber ERG in Paris, I immediately felt my heart and intuition drawing me to share my personal story with these women along with a call to action. I had never shared my story of coming out of the closet in a public forum like that, including how I nearly committed suicide. I announced to them I was asked to speak on women's safety and gender-based violence, but I instead felt compelled to tell them my personal story as a Queer woman. The currents of my heart were drawing me to this very moment to share. They didn't stop me.

I shared my personal story—the story that I share with you in this book. The story of that day when I nearly took my life, but I didn't stop there. I told them telling my husband at the time that I was gay and wanted a divorce was one of the most painful things I ever had to do. I told them about the stories of my coming out to family and friends. I certainly experienced unconditional love and acceptance from some, but I also shared with them the pain, rejection, and the hate I experienced.

I told them the stories of everything from outright rejection in responses to silent rejection. You know the kind of rejection where your friends just quietly disappear and become unresponsive. I told them stories of hate from being called names like faggot to receiving threats of harm, not just once, but throughout my journey. There were many days I felt so alone and just wanted to be treated like every human being deserves. It was so important during that time to have people encircle me with love and affirmation, people that were willing to use their voices and take genuine action on behalf of me—to stand purposefully with me and for everyone in the community. One of those people was my ex-husband after witnessing firsthand the harm that happens.

I shared that I felt safe and protected and those people who showed me genuine care and support were instrumental in helping me become fully who I am with confidence. That tremendous support and confidence in turn led to my ability to make the impact I was able to make. I then told them about what was happening to the LGBTQ+ community in their own country—to their own people. I told them about the statistics, but I also shared stories from their own country that local NGOs had shared with me. You could have heard a pin drop in the room, and many were crying. I told them I could see that what I was sharing was breaking their hearts, but I also needed them to be outraged by it. I needed them to be angry. "This is not just my community. This is your community. These are your people," I reminded them.

I shared that there was one woman sitting in this room who had dedicated her heart and time trying to lead the Uber Pride ERG in France, trying to get people involved in meaningful action on behalf of people like me and on behalf of the LGBTQ+ community in their country. I told them I heard people hadn't exactly been lining up to get involved and help her.

"We need protectors, and we need allies to create spaces for us to be and feel safe, to feel belonging, and to feel human. We need people to fight for us to have the same freedoms, safety, and rights for members of the LGBTQ+ community that all people deserve. We will continue to fight this fight alone, but we want each of you to join us. We need you. I need you," I told them as I extended one hand towards them and placed the other over my heart. Then I asked each person in that room to please not stand by while members of their community were being harmed. "We should never stand by when anyone is being harmed," I reminded them. I told them I needed them to rise up and that I was there to support them and tell them how they could help.

Using my voice and telling my personal story in France was not easy. Talking about the painful parts is never easy, but it created human connection and created the opportunity for magic to happen. It inspired change and ignited action. As a result, a majority of those women were moved to use their personal power to take meaningful action.

Many got involved in the French Uber Pride ERG after my talk and got involved in supporting the LGBTQ+ community outside of Uber, working directly with organizations. The PR, policy, and product teams drove partnerships and developed education and initiatives focused on the LGBTQ+ community. The French team became a model for other regions. Some of those women in that room that day have told me that they have never forgotten that moment when I spoke to them.

It wasn't that they didn't care, but I helped create a space and a moment where they could truly see me and see a community that needed them. It fostered empathy. It created a shared connection and a space where they could see it was not just my community, but it was their community—their people. I also created a space that helped them identify and learn how they could take action, and they did just that! They took action that drove significant change.

I'll never forget what happened the day after I shared my personal story. The woman who was leading Uber Pride in France and had sought me out for my help came up to me and gave me a huge hug. "People are coming to me; they're joining and getting involved!" she told me excitedly. Tears began to roll down my face, and that evening in my hotel I cried deep from my core. A deep cry that recalled the pain of my journey but also a cry of gratitude for the genuine care and hope of others. I found purpose and power in the sharing of my personal story—my own story of heartbreak and hope.

Up to that point, I had only leveraged the stories of others and some of my experiences. In Paris that day, I learned that there was value and tremendous power in sharing more of my own personal story, and I haven't stopped since. There is personal power and purpose in your lived experience when you use your own voice to deliver the story, both the good and difficult parts. Power to bring human connection. Power to create community. Power to spark and ignite personal power and collective action in others.

To my French family and colleagues who worked with me and always welcomed and embraced me at Uber. You know who you are. Thank you for listening and creating a safe place for me to share my story. Thank you for your genuine care. Thank you for your actions. You helped me come to believe in the power of my own story, which helped me move into an even greater understanding of my own purpose and the personal power within myself.

Ask for what you want—what the world needs

When you find what is breaking your heart, when you identify what is breaking the heart of others, when you identify the desires of your heart, are you using your voice to ask for what you want—what the world needs? If you don't use your voice to ask for it, to manifest it, you really can't expect to get it. You can't expect things to change or be addressed. You can't expect to get what you want and desire.

What increases your likelihood of getting what you want? Asking for it. Manifesting it. Saying it out loud. What increases the likelihood of getting what the world needs? It starts with raising your individual voice towards solutions and asking for actions to happen. I don't know how many times I have spoken with individuals and groups who have identified a need or want but are afraid to ask for it or have given up after one negative response or failure and then don't know how to move forward. You must learn to have the courage to use your voice and take action for yourself before you can successfully do it for others.

Often it is fear, a scarcity mindset, limiting thoughts, and/ or a feeling of not being enough that stops us from using our voices and taking action. We don't even give the others or the universe a chance to show up for us when we don't ask—when we don't use our voices to say it out loud. If you are unsure of what you want, what you want to manifest, or what is needed, ask yourself. Have you taken the time to ask yourself? Sit with it, reflect on what matters most and what is breaking your heart, and see what comes to you. The answer is in you. The pathway will come to you.

If the decision has been made or landed, and you feel strongly it was not the best decision, you still have the opportunity to disrupt the landing and impact. That can be a personal experience, a professional experience, or a societal problem. Let me give you a professional example. I recall when I was at Uber, and we went through a round of layoffs. A manager came to me and told me members of my women's safety and gender-based violence programmatic team were going to be laid off. I knew those actions would have a detrimental impact on the programs, partnerships, and support my team provided across the business; ultimately, adversely affecting both the business and safety.

I've found along my journey, most people just do what they are told and are good soldiers rather than asking questions, and if needed, challenging the status quo. You also can't believe when there are many levels of management and operations, that what you do, the value you bring, and the impact it has on people and consumers has been fully and accurately communicated or is fully understood at the highest levels of an organization.

I asked a lot of questions about what informed the decision and gathered as much information as possible. I offered up alternative solutions and had a business case I believed in strongly. I asked that it be evaluated, and the layoffs of my team members be reconsidered. The answer did not change. The layoffs were going to happen. I was told the decision had already landed but I knew decisions could be overturned no matter the odds.

I decided to go straight to the executive who oversaw the entire division at the time. Now, I also was transparent with my own manager and many other senior level managers about what I was going to do. Not one of them said they would do the same thing, and few even admitted to being afraid to do something similar even though we had a so-called open-door policy. I made certain I acknowledged my manager's contributions to help maintain trust and respect and communicated why it was important for me to be the one to deliver my business case along with the message of my heart. They understood and in return supported me and acknowledged my courage.

For the executive involved, I asked permission to speak to them and took the approach that I felt was important to provide additional information to them that I believed was very crucial in helping inform the decisions that were being considered by the business. They agreed to meet with me in person.

I went into that meeting with two things. A strong business case and the message of my heart. It's been my experience that you will have greater success getting what you desire when you bring both. I didn't criticize management. I didn't criticize the decision by management. You want to know what happened? I came out of that meeting with an overturned decision. My team and my safety program would continue.

Here are a few action steps that helped me achieve my mission that day:

- Begin and end from a place of respect and integrity.

- Demonstrate genuine acknowledgment and care not only for people/consumers but also for the people who follow you and work beside you.

- Use your voice in every moment of the experience to communicate what you want, what you believe is needed to best serve others, and the message of your heart.

- Know what you're talking about. Know the language and current state of the business.

- Predict what questions will be asked, and already have the answers.

- Build a case for action and verbalize it. Identify solutions including how you will execute on it.

- Verbalize the positive impact potential and back it with data if you can.

- Weave it into their current objectives and connect it to what they care about.

- Build the case but also go for the heart.

🕯 Deliver the message yourself, including the message of your heart in person if possible. There is personal power in you and your purpose but also in human connection.

Is it always going to work? No, it won't 100% of the time, but you will never know unless you ask for what you want, use your voice to manifest it, and elevate the need, follow your intuition, and move through your fear. That goes for yourself and the impact you want to make for others in this world.

How long do you keep asking? How long do you keep manifesting? How long do you keep taking action? As long as your heart and intuition compels you. Follow where it leads you even if the pathway is not totally clear and risky. Use your voice, find your courage, act upon it, and watch the disruption happen in both your personal and professional life.

Don't keep your head down and your voice silent

Women and members of historically marginalized communities often don't feel seen and heard where we are at, whether in our homes, our communities, or our places of work. People, governments, and organizations are not always fully supporting our well-being and unique needs and are not looking to those with lived experience to help develop the right solutions. We can't choose to remain silent, keep our heads down, and keep our most powerful tool hidden. Our voice is a superhero power that not only inspires others but can create safety for yourself and others. It can drive impactful change.

There is also always going to be somebody who hasn't heard the message of your heart. One of the best communications leaders I worked with always said repetition never spoils the prayer, and messages take time to sink in. Keep repeating the same message over and over again. Find out new and interesting ways to say the same thing. Repeat it over and over again.

I say find ways to weave the message of your heart into the fabric and design of all you do. You are here to use your voice and deliver the message of your heart. Not the message of any institution. Not the message of any other person. You are here to be fully who you are, and you have within you the personal power to inspire and empower others, igniting collective power to make bold, disruptive change that brings us closer to our shared visions.

Now, maybe founding and leading a non-profit organization doesn't suit you. You may or may not see yourself as an activist. You may or may not see yourself as a leader. Maybe where you are right now is you just want things to be better. Better in your own personal life and better in the lives of others. Maybe you have become complacent. Just keeping your head down, doing your job, and getting through the day not trying to cause waves, but also not believing you can make a difference while you—while we all—watch much of our progress like our foundational rights being stripped away. You question how your one voice, your lived experience, and the message of your heart could ever bring forth positive change where there is pain, helplessness, and what feels like continuous challenges for yourself and so many. I still believe there is a superhero waiting to be unleashed in you.

Let me tell you about Alex. She, like many women, assumed she would get married and have a family. People always painted a very positive picture of pregnancy. We all know the story and expectations: You find the person you love, get married, and then the next natural step is to get pregnant and have children.

It's this beautiful fairy tale that also gave birth to an untruth—the misconception that it would all happen easily. No one talked about the full context of trying to create another human being. No one had ever had the conversation with Alex about the likelihood of miscarriage and pregnancy loss. As women, we rarely share those stories of struggle and loss, but there came a point where Alex knew she had to share her powerful story and experience to demonstrate the importance of having autonomy over our bodies and the need for holistic well-being care.

"I was closing in on 30 years old, so my then-husband and I decided that we wanted to start a family," Alex told me. "But for me it was very difficult to get pregnant and then stay pregnant once I conceived and my difficulties led me down a long and painful path of being hyper watchful of what my body was doing, keeping track often hourly for the optimal conditions for conception, often conceiving... but then failing to keep the pregnancy," she explained.

It felt to her that no matter what she did to try to maintain her pregnancies, nothing ever worked. That planted a seed of hopelessness, and psychological and emotional safety began to erode for her. Everything she had been led to believe painted a different picture than what she was experiencing. "I began to question myself not only physically but on a much deeper level, wondering what was wrong with me and why I wasn't normal, like everyone else seemed to be," Alex shared. "Once I started to have the pregnancy loss issues I had, I just lost that pure sense of joy and wonder many women start with on their journey to becoming a mother. Instead, fear set in, and I began to question my own value and worth."

After Alex and her then-husband decided to start their family, it took two years for Alex to get pregnant. Weeks into the pregnancy she began to bleed, and that first pregnancy lasted only seven weeks before she miscarried. This first experience with the difficulties that often come with conception and pregnancy shocked Alex, and the impact was adverse beyond what she could have imagined. It was a spontaneous loss, and it was unknown what caused the miscarriage.

Not only was the emotional impact devastating, but the physical effects after her miscarriage were excruciatingly painful. As a standard medical procedure to induce her and pass everything, her OBGYN gave her Misoprostol and Mifepristone, also known as an abortion pill. She wouldn't stop bleeding and ended up in the ER on the verge of hemorrhaging. She had to have an emergency medical intervention with a D&C (Dilation and Curettage). "After that miscarriage, I couldn't go to the bathroom for years without checking for blood," Alex recalled.

That was the first but not the last miscarriage for Alex. "My second miscarriage happened in early 2011 and my third miscarriage happened in late 2011. They were both similarly devastating situations with serious medical complications associated. The second time I miscarried I was 13 weeks pregnant, and, as many will understand, I thought I was 'safe' because my pregnancy had made it past the first trimester. I remember a deep emotional and physical feeling of relief once I passed that first trimester mark... and I also let myself feel excited, believing this time the pregnancy would be successful," Alex remembered. "Even when I started to bleed at 13 weeks, I tried to convince myself that it could be normal. But it wasn't. I lost that pregnancy and on top of that, the pregnancy was initially diagnosed as a molar pregnancy, which is essentially a cancerous mass in the uterus," she told me. It was a similar experience for her then with significant medical issues and intervention.

There was nothing she could have done to avoid it. She had to have an immediate D&C again and go through various tests to confirm whether or not the pregnancy was a molar pregnancy. The same paperwork you fill out for an elected abortion is the same paperwork you fill out for an emergency D&C. There she was filing the paperwork out again. She described the whole process as "ugly." Not just the paperwork, not just the procedure, but the unnecessary rhetoric around the concept of an abortion also impacted her.

And although ultimately the pregnancy turned out not to be a molar pregnancy, during the time Alex was waiting for test results to confirm the status she had several conversations with her doctor about the treatment and process following a molar pregnancy, including possibly being required to wait two years before trying to conceive again. "It was such a dark time for me, and most of it is a blur," Alex recalls. "But even when I think about that period today so many years later, tears come to my eyes immediately."

Alex's third miscarriage occurred at about seven weeks, and it was a life-threatening ectopic pregnancy. Ectopic pregnancies pose serious health concerns and again she had to terminate the pregnancy immediately. Once again, Alex had to go in for a D&C. She recalls the same paperwork and the same pain.

Ectopic pregnancies are the type of pregnancy that we hear about so much now since the overturning of Roe versus Wade and the resulting lack of access to critical reproductive care and abortion. The termination of some pregnancies, such as ectopic pregnancies, through abortion is a life-saving procedure that doctors are now not able to simply make the decision to perform. Instead, doctors have to talk to attorneys in back rooms to determine if they can legally perform the procedure while the woman's life is on the line and precious time is lost. This abortion procedure that was life-saving for Alex is now illegal to perform in countless states across the U.S.

After the third miscarriage, her OBGYN referred Alex to a fertility specialist. She was ultimately able to conceive and keep a pregnancy, but this level of intervention included invasive hormonal treatment, medication, and shots. The emotional and psychological impacts on Alex continued through this treatment.

The day Roe versus Wade was overturned, Alex felt the blow, like many, to her physical, emotional, and psychological safety. She describes the hopelessness, the fear, the anger, and the feeling that nothing was ever going to change. She describes the immediate impact as broadly psychological with the shocking disbelief that the U.S. Supreme Court had the ability to take back what were fundamental rights to manage one's own reproductive space and ultimately their own bodies.

"For me, it was a clear statement regarding how women and our autonomy are not valued in our society. I was terrified of what could happen next with women's rights, the rights of the LGBTQ+ community, and beyond. And in addition to the shock and disbelief, I felt an immediate feeling of defeat and fatigue," she recalls. "It was as if the air had been knocked out of me."

Many saw the U.S. Supreme Court's decision as yet another way of controlling women and their reproductive space, and it made it seem like the progress with regard to gender equality got a kick in the gut. The huge, sweeping impact was an incredible move backwards. Alex felt initially that there was no point continuing the fight when so much ground had been lost. She was not alone in these feelings. So many of us felt the same.

Alex was not in a place to be pregnant again, but she knew that so many were. Alex became energized from the immediate ability to connect with other women and impacted members of the LGBTQ+ community that were currently impacted or would be impacted in the future by these laws. Alex was galvanized to fight for and find ways to provide access to reproductive healthcare and abortion that could help others right where she was at.

"In my role, I had already been working on a fund for the prior few months where my employer would support abortion access for its employees in the state where I lived. This was in response to my state being the first to modify its laws to restrict access to abortion in anticipation of the overturning of Roe versus Wade. I was also seeing many other states take steps to follow suit. To say it was concerning is a serious understatement," Alex explained.

Alex, an attorney by trade and beloved leader within her global corporation, went to the company benefits manager to review the company sponsored benefits and find ways to create access to reproductive healthcare in support of impacted women. Her goal was to rally others, review and modify internal policies, and ensure the company benefits carriers and their policies included coverage for reproductive healthcare, abortion access, and related incidentals for all employees no matter the state they resided in.

This would include updated employer sponsored health benefits and coverage of related costs like travel to another state that did not restrict access to the necessary care. It was important the language was clear so there was no gray space with abortion. Alex discovered in her investigation that her employer's current benefits only covered medically necessary abortions and only for those employers who elected healthcare coverage through the employer's health and welfare benefits plans. There was a concerning gap when it came to non-medically necessary or referral abortions as well as elective abortions, and there was a gap in coverage for employees and dependents who did not elect the company's healthcare benefits.

Alex helped to drive the campaign that resulted in the creation of a fund to cover the gaps she identified and be inclusive of the myriad of circumstances that employees and their dependents faced that led to the need for full access to reproductive healthcare, access to and coverage of the costs for abortion services and aftercare, as well as financial assistance for related travel for both the impacted employee or dependent and an individual to support them. In response to the successful program that Alex supported and developed, numerous other companies and in-house and outside counsel outreached to Alex to ask her how she did it and get her partnership in creating similar programs.

Alex's personal story, the message of her heart and the actions she took, had a direct impact on not only changing and improving programs and policies to address the unique needs of women and non-binary individuals, but it also created access and a space where physical, emotional, and physiological safety could be fostered and experienced by many. She didn't keep her voice silent and look what happened.

Her story is a story of loss, but also one of courage, hope, and individual action that ignited meaningful change. She continues to follow the currents of her heart and drive change but the biggest impact for her has come from creating a practice of first choosing to value and prioritize herself and making bold moves in pursuit of her heart's desires, all resulting in her becoming a better version of self. She is someone who still struggles with those voices of self-doubt daily, but she moves more and more to embracing her value and the superhero within her, using her voice and personal power to create change for herself and others.

Your powerful voice, your story of lived experience, and your actions can create momentum and movement in getting the desires of your heart, the desires of many of our hearts, and the change the world may need in what breaks our hearts. If it doesn't happen the way you envisioned, you will find your actions will instead provide clarity and opportunity for a next step or new path forward.

Pathways will appear like magic that you could have never imagined that can provide opportunities to unleash your superhero power to achieve the desires of your heart, create meaningful impact in what breaks your heart, and activate and inspire others.

Raise your head, raise your voice, raise your story, and rise up unleashing the power within you.

Chapter 5 activators

Reflection questions:

➤➤ What is one area, personally or professionally, where I can use my voice where I have previously chosen to remain silent? Where are the currents of my heart drawing me to use my voice?

➤➤ What is the message of my heart? What are a few things about my personal story that I often don't share that have been pivotal in shaping who I am today?

Personal power tip: Weave your personal story and the message of your heart into all you do. Make it personal. Take people on the journey with you using your voice and your personal story. Share both the struggles and the wins. Share the heartache. The celebrations. The history. Your history. Your lived experience. Share what it is like to walk every day in your shoes. Share your fears, your strengths, your vulnerability. Weave your personal story and the message of your heart into your conversations, your communications, your presentations, your experiences with people. Stories of personal, lived experience are some of the most powerful and purposeful tools for change that we have. That includes your own personal story as well as the stories of others. It truly brings a human connection and opportunity to change hearts. It creates space for others to feel safe and supported.

Unleash your superhero: Buy or create something connected to your superhero. It can be a framed quote, poster, drawing, or figurine. Anything that is representative of that superhero. Place the item in a space or place you frequently spend time such as your office and/or home as a symbolic reminder when you need encouragement in knowing there is a superhero within you. When people see it and ask about it, tell them how you relate and connect to that superhero. I have a Captain America shield hanging on my wall. It's an attention grabber on Zoom calls!

Manifestation affirmation: My voice and my story are powerful. My voice and my lived experience create a unique, meaningful impact in my life and in the world. I will not be silenced. I will use my voice and share my story.

Lay down your safety

You will face ridicule and criticism

I believe that to create impactful change in our own personal lives and social change in the world we must also be willing to lay down our safety. It's an inconvenient truth and a reality in particular for women, members of the LGBTQ+ community, or other historically marginalized groups. When we choose to use our voices, when we choose to challenge the status quo, when we choose to deliver the message of our hearts, when we choose to stand up for others like ourselves, when we take a stand against the people and the systems that oppress us, when we choose to ignite our personal power, it will often require us to lay down our safety.

Now what do I mean? People have become complacent, living in fear, and many don't believe their lives or systems can be changed. They don't believe their personal power matters. Many have even created for themselves a false sense of safety. They have become good soldiers, refusing to challenge the status quo, and just do what they are told even though it may not be or feel right. That false sense of safety provides an element of comfort, but we don't grow, and change, if any, happens slowly. We remain unfulfilled. The reality is there is no real safety in silence and inaction.

I also want to acknowledge what is also true. The truth is if you are a woman or member of a historically marginalized group, your emotional, psychological, and physical safety may be adversely impacted when you use your voice and take meaningful steps to create positive change in your life and the lives of others because many of us are not living or work-ing in safe environments that foster genuine care, openness, candid feedback, and inclusion. It is a courageous act of service to lay down both your perceived and actual safety for others, but it is also the only pathway to big, bold, individual, and societal change in an unjust world.

Let's talk about what happens when you lay down your safety. Expect to be criticized and ridiculed when you lay down your safety, particularly if you work for an organization or for a leader that has not created safe spaces to raise your voice and provide them with feedback even if they don't agree with you. Women often face a double bind and microaggressions. How often have you heard a woman leader criticized, and their assertiveness called aggressive or angry?

Studies have shown that microaggressions—such having one's judgment questioned—are more commonly experienced by women of color, women with disabilities, and LGBTQ+ women than men, and women overall in professional settings. Women also receive negative personality criticism, such as being called bossy or told to watch their tone in around 75% of performance reviews. Men, on the other hand, rarely do.[1]

The reality also is that many of us are still impacted by a patriarchal system that views women and members of marginalized communities much more harshly when we speak up and challenge ideas and actions. I can't tell you how many times throughout my career I have been described and witnessed many other women described as aggressive, angry, brazen, and a host of other negative words mostly by men. One of these days I will have all those words on a wall somewhere!

Don't let those words limit, stop, or silence you. You can still be considerate while being confident, authentic, direct, and clear even in a place of disagreement or unjust criticism. Not everyone will agree with you, like you, or share your values. This can send many people right back into silence, particularly if they question their own value. It can also be very hard and painful when the unjust criticism comes from other women and members of our own communities.

As difficult as it might be, you have to remember it is not about you. Nothing others do is about you, so work on not taking it personally. You don't know where people are along their own personal journey or the trauma they may have faced and not worked to address. Their own insecurities and woundedness may be surfaced and directed at you and they also may have a lack of knowledge and understanding. Some of the best advice that was given to me as a police officer by trauma-informed experts was that without help, hurt people hurt people.

I've also learned that people who are not comfortable in their own skin and are not living authentically, will often not be comfortable in your authentic, confident presence unless they are open to self-growth and achieving greater self-awareness. Pay attention to their non-verbal behavior and your own intuition. You will feel and sense it, and they will fear you may recognize their lack of authenticity. In reaction, sometimes they may avoid you, unjustly criticize you, and even try to undermine you.

When you hear the words they use to describe you and the unjust criticism, just ask yourself what is true and stay grounded in who you know yourself to be. You are not how they may describe you. That's one way that people and systems stop us from elevating others and creating the societal change that needs to happen. We not only allow the internal limiting voices to distract us and stop us at times, but we also allow the external limiting voices to stop us as well. Don't let them!

Now, people may have different opinions and that's okay. Maybe there is something for you to learn from engaging with them or your engagement may open them up to greater understanding and acceptance. Offering information, sharing your story, giving people an opportunity to hear a different perspective, and receiving an opportunity to hear another perspective, may also create opportunities for human connections and new allies.

However, don't allow anyone to abuse you (in word or action), and don't get caught up in putting all your energy into convincing people to care as much as you do about yourself, social issues, and doing the right thing when they have made it clear through word or action that they don't. You don't need everyone to like you, you don't need everyone to agree with you, and you don't need everyone to care in order to drive impactful change.

Be careful. Don't be fooled by some of them. It's been my experience that sometimes people can be extremely challenging. Sometimes people do a very good job of pretending to be your ally. They can sometimes be charismatic and put on a really good performance. They sometimes appear and work very hard on an outward appearance that is not authentically who they truly are. Follow your intuition when engaging with them. You can sense inauthenticity.

Don't allow other people's opinions, criticisms, inauthenticity, or actions shape who you are and the meaningful work you want to do. Don't allow people to place their own limiting thoughts upon you. I don't know how many times I've taken a stand on an issue, shared my vision or my audacious dreams, and some people have responded with, "I can't get on board with that," or they say, "That's just crazy, there's no way you can do that," or "That's just too big."

Don't let people's disbelief, unjust criticisms, opinions, or even dislike of you stop you when you choose to use your voice and take actions on behalf of yourself or others, especially when your intentions are rooted in integrity, authenticity, genuine care for people, and doing the right thing in what breaks your heart. Keep moving forward. Keep raising your voice. Keep taking a stand. Lay down your safety. There will be everyday superheroes who respond differently and join you, responding with, "Yes, let's do this!"

Criticism and ridicule are tools used by people and systems that continue to silence and oppress us. It won't always feel good, and it won't always feel safe when you raise your voice and take action. But, when you stay grounded in authenticity, what is true, what matters most, and you follow the currents of what is breaking your heart, choosing to lay down your safety and use your voice can not only create positive change for yourself but it will also inspire others to join you.

The collective voices will get louder, a circle of safety will be created, and the actions and impact will be ignited and will spread! Trust me. You will quickly find you are not alone, and there are others waiting to hear the voice that echoes what is in their heart and helps ignite personal power and action, creating pathways that result in opportunities to be fully who we are, achieve the desires of our hearts and make an impactful difference in the world individually and together.

Discrimination and retaliation are likely

When you lay down your safety and do the things I've discussed in this book, it can result in individuals and organizations driving meaningful change separately and together. However, if you are a woman, a member of the LGBTQ+ community, or other marginalized group, it can also lead to discrimination and retaliation, especially in the workplace.

We have worked so hard to achieve representation, but systems and institutions continue to try and silence us. We certainly have come a long way with civil rights laws and workplace laws that were created to protect us, but retaliation and discrimination still happens.

I've talked to countless women and other members of historically marginalized groups who have challenged the status quo, raised their voices, elevated voices and concerns, spoken out against harm, or just simply regularly brought new ideas to the table and provided feedback and then found themselves being retaliated and/or discriminated against. Too often, they have no idea it is happening until it's too late, and they are exited from an organization. It can be subtle or blatant, but I've often seen the more subtle approach.

Ashwiyaa, like everyone who starts a new job, was so excited to land a leadership role at a large company. She signed the employment contracts presented to her without hesitation placing most of her focus on her title, salary, equity, and job description. She couldn't wait to start her new leadership role!

The first year went smoothly and she and her approach were well received. Her influential executive manager encouraged her to share her ideas and concerns candidly, and she did. Her team expanded, and she felt her executive manager supported her and had her back.

She had outstanding reviews and feedback from her manager. She also became a trusted advisor for executives. That was a track record she had at previous jobs that had continued. As she entered her second year, her influence expanded as a trusted voice for marginalized individuals and groups in her organization. She had deep knowledge about workplace safety and inclusion through her lived experience as an Indigenous woman.

Through her work and relationships, Ashwiyaa became aware of harm that was occurring within the organization. She raised her concerns to her leadership, offering her ideas on how to make improvements and take proactive steps going forward. Leadership responded to her that they appreciated her bringing the concerns forward along with her ideas about resolution for them. They said they were on board to address the issues appropriately and would leverage her expertise.

"I believe that speaking out about those concerns was the beginning of the end, even though my management appeared to respond positively," Ashwiyaa recalled. "As the weeks went by, I started to slowly feel invisible. I was starting to be left out of meetings and discussions I would normally be a part of. I had this gut feeling that my voice was being ignored and my ideas were no longer being heard. I was being left out of cross-functional projects I would normally be involved in. Leaders were canceling one-to-ones with me," she said. "Whenever I would question these things, I always got a 'fine' surface-level response, but I could just feel it—that something was really off."

Ashwiyaa then heard from peers that her performance was being criticized by leadership in front of others. She was shocked because she had never received that feedback directly. Out of nowhere, after returning from a leave of absence, she was put on a performance improvement plan. She began to feel as if the organization was trying to push her out. She no longer felt safe, valued, or as if she belonged at the organization.

"Within a few weeks of being put on that performance improvement plan, I was fired. It was like clockwork, or something inevitable that you can see coming but you can't stop," Ashwiyaa told me. "I had never been fired from a job before in my career and I was in shock. I knew what happened to me was not right, but I knew I needed help to fight back. So, I found an attorney." Ashwiyaa quickly learned she had been retaliated against. When her attorney asked to see her employment contract, her attorney told her that she had signed a mandatory arbitration clause in her employment documents, which would greatly impact her situation. Although this was the first she was aware of such a clause or even that she had signed off on it, Ashwiyaa quickly learned for the first time in her career what mandatory arbitration was and how these programs silence women just like her.

Mandatory, or forced, arbitration is a program that most private sector employers in the U.S. use as the method of dispute resolution for claims that the employee may have against the employer. The most common disputes that are subject to forced arbitration in the employment context are discrimination, harassment, and retaliation in all of its forms (except, as related to claims of sexual harassment and sexual assault with the passage of the Ending Forced Arbitration Act of Sexual Harassment and Sexual Assault Act, or EFASHASA, in 2022 which amended the Federal Arbitration Act).

A forced arbitration clause compels you into a secret chamber where your complaint will be heard, instead of allowing you to file a public lawsuit. Let's say something bad happens to you at work and you report it. Instead of bringing the case to a jury of your peers, which is your 7th Amendment right, an arbiter, often selected by your employer, will hear the dispute and make a final and binding decision about the outcome.

Employers favor arbitration over litigation in federal or state court because arbitration proceedings are private—not a matter of public record. Arbitration can be marginally less expensive regarding costs and fees, and presenting a matter before a single arbitrator that is typically a legal professional significantly reduces the risk of a runaway jury that awards damages to a plaintiff in empathy to their experience in the employment relationship (rather than an arbitrator who is typically assumed to render a less emotional and more legally-founded decision). The deck is stacked against you. The arbiter almost always rules in favor of the company. Employers prevail in more than 97% of arbitration disputes.[2]

An estimated 56% of private sector non-union U.S. employees, approximately 60 million Americans, are subject to mandatory arbitration by their employers.[3] It is growing exponentially. By 2024, it is projected that, absent Congressional action, 80% of all private sector non-union employers will force arbitration agreements on their U.S. employees as a condition of employment.[4]

They also include non-disclosure agreements and employee-mandated confidentiality that silence you. When employees go through arbitration to resolve workplace disputes, employers should not be able to force employees to keep what happened to them, or how it was resolved, a secret.

Forced employment arbitration has a significant impact on employee's rights—and most impacted employees are not even aware. While historically national policy has been to favor arbitration for the reasons noted above, my experience and the experience of so many others is that employers routinely use forced arbitration as a way to ensure that employees remain silent regarding employment concerns, keeping employee complaints outside public legal forums such as federal and state courts.

The impact is significant for current and future employees in workplaces that don't address and remediate issues of discrimination, harassment, and retaliation because it prohibits employees from speaking out about their experience and supports toxic workplace culture without visible, vocal, public repercussions to the employer.

All employees deserve the right to speak truthfully about their experiences, and we know that women, LGBTQ+ individuals, and other marginalized groups are disproportionately impacted by mandatory employment arbitration with even greater impact when an individual intersects with multiple marginalized identities.

Look through your employee contract before signing and look for legal terms such as arbitration, dispute, confidentiality, non-disparagement, and non-disclosure. Clauses forcing people to sign away their rights to go to court are often buried in fine print in employment contracts and terms of service.

Find out if your employer has it. Grassroots efforts by employees led to employers such as Google, recognizing the adverse impact on groups, and completely removing it for employees. I was a member of a group of employees who helped convince Uber to proactively remove it for sexual harassment and assault years before legislation was passed to amend the Federal Arbitration Act. We need more companies to lead and take this impactful step! You may be able to rally fellow employees to get your company to recognize the importance of taking similar steps.

Many companies will refuse to remove it, but you can still take meaningful action. One way is to help pass legislation to end forced arbitration. There is current U.S. legislation being proposed to remove it for racial and age discrimination. It was successfully done for sexual harassment and assault in 2022. Visit the National Women's Law Center, Lift Our Voices, and The Purple Method online who have been working on workplace fairness issues including ending all forced arbitration. Let's expand it to all forms of discrimination and retaliation.

Employees who are subject to retaliation and discrimination and other violations of their rights should be able to choose to share their stories with colleagues to discuss ideas for collective action instead of being silenced by employer-mandated confidentiality and arbitration. Ensuring that women and marginalized groups are not forced by their employers into mandatory arbitration and confidentiality is critical for creating safe, transparent, and inclusive workplaces, where harm is never kept secret.

If you feel you are being retaliated against or discriminated against, trust your intuition. If something feels off, it probably is. Talk to your community groups and friends outside of work and let them know what is happening. Affirmation and support can be reassuring and help you move forward. Seek out advice from an employment litigation attorney who specializes in these matters. Seek counseling support. The emotional and physical toll can be intense, and support will be critical as the process can be overwhelming, long, and stressful.

What broke Ashwiyaa's heart and so many others has become a purpose and a movement they are a part of to help remove forced arbitration, so people never have to experience what happened to them. They are raising awareness and helping expand a movement to remove this tool from corporate playbooks that is often used to harm women and marginalized groups.

Ashwiyaa found a new opportunity that embraces her voice and passion. Retaliation and harm may have happened, but it didn't stop her or her purpose. When we lay down our safety, we will also find that we create safety. People rise up together for a cause creating a new circle of safety and opportunities for individual and social change.

It's a crucial part of activating movement

Laying down your safety is a crucial part of igniting and activating collective action and movement. Grassroots movements that have truly driven big, bold, social change started with one person willing to lay down their safety and then many more followed. People take notice when you lay down your safety—because most people don't.

It takes tremendous courage, but it is often the catalyst that can start a movement. Most people just do what they're told, are fearful to speak up, may lack understanding, or may lack knowledge on what actions they can take. Some people are followers and need a leader. There also can be real potential for harm to people. When you find the courage and you step into that space where you lay down your safety, others will take notice, and this is what it will do—it will inspire others. It will ignite and activate personal power in others. It fuels courage and ignites fire in others, and they will join you. It leads to collective action. The more people that join, the larger the circle of safety becomes. Some people will never be leaders. That just doesn't feel comfortable to them, or they feel very alone. Sometimes they just need somebody to follow, to give them permission, and once somebody takes that step and begins to lead, others will follow. Many will also step up to lead with them and the followers will be activated because they will feel protected and safe in the circle of safety that is being created.

I believe that when you're willing to lay down your safety, it creates the catalyst that leads to big, bold movement. Your action may be the one action needed. It may only take one action of laying down your safety, whether it is physical safety or your psychological safety, that could lead to more moments of courage and a movement of change. One of my favorite examples of laying down safety for others is the story of Rosa Parks.

In 1955, Rosa Parks was a seamstress in Montgomery, Alabama and was already very active in the Civil Rights Movement. She led the youth division at the Montgomery branch of the National Association for the Advancement of Colored People (NAACP). On December 1, 1955, she boarded a bus after work to go home. Shortly after as more people got on the bus, the section reserved for white passengers had filled and she was told to move to the back of the bus. And then, as even more white passengers got on the bus, Parks was told to give up her seat in the colored section for a white passenger. She refused the bus driver's order to leave a row of four seats in the colored section. She refused to vacate a seat on a bus in favor of a white passenger.[5] She refused. She laid down her safety.

In her autobiography, Parks said her actions were intentional: "I was not tired physically, or no more tired than I usually was at the end of a working day. I was not old, although some people have an image of me as being old then. I was 42. No, the only tired I was, was tired of giving in."[5]

She was arrested and lost her job, but her courageous act of defiance was the driving force for a movement. Her act of defiance sparked the Montgomery Bus Boycott, one of the largest social movements in history. It inspired a young Martin Luther King, Jr. who would lead the boycott. The movement resulted in the enforcement of a U.S. Supreme Court ruling that public bus segregation is unconstitutional. It also propelled both King and Parks into the national spotlight as civil rights leaders.

Parks said her anger over the lynching of 14-year-old Emmett Till and the failure to bring his killers to justice was what inspired her actions on December 1, 1955—actions that ignited to a movement.

"I had no idea when I refused to give up my seat on that Montgomery bus that my small action would help put an end to the segregation laws in the South," said Parks.[5]

Responding to what angered and broke her heart, Parks courageously laid down her safety and used her voice and actions in service of herself and many others just like her. One of those actions was the catalyst to inspire multitudes of people into a movement that drove incredible social change.

Her actions helped raise international awareness of racism in the U.S. Her refusal on the Montgomery bus that day and her subsequent arrest is considered to be the catalyst that fueled the Civil Rights Movement. She would continue to fight and remain active in the Civil Rights Movement, would go on to join the movement for fair housing, and would also go on to advocate on issues such as job discrimination, education, and affordable housing. Her life and activism in the Civil Rights Movement would continue to help drive change and inspire countless lives even after her death at 92.

What experiences or observations are angering you? What are you witnessing around you that is breaking your heart? What is sitting with you right now and keeps coming back to you? What is showing up in your reflection and is calling to you? Ignore the criticism and limiting thoughts that may be surfacing. Instead, feel the currents of your heart and follow them. They can lead you to an action that transforms your life or the life of another. They may also ignite a movement in your home, in your workplace, in your community, or beyond what you could ever envision. It can create a circle of safety as others join and support you.

The currents of your heart may lead you to a small action or a big action. But what I know to be true is sometimes what feels like a small action quickly becomes a superhero action. When you lay down your safety with integrity and courage, in service of yourself, in service of others, and in service of the greater good of humanity, people will notice and be inspired to take similar just and courageous, superhero actions.

After you do it, keep it up. Make it a practice. Then look around. Look behind you. Look beside you. You won't be alone for very long.

Chapter 6 activators

🔥 **Reflection questions**:

➤➤ How have I allowed other people's opinions, criticisms, inauthenticity, or actions shape who I am and the meaningful work I want to do?

➤➤ What experiences or observations are angering me? What am I witnessing that is breaking my heart? What would I alone be willing to lay my safety down for or if others were willing to join me?

🔥 **Personal power tip**: This tip is for those who are current leaders and are the rising leaders of tomorrow. It's for both leaders and followers who are tired of giving in. Women and members of historically marginalized communities who feel the pull to intervene and step in with action rather than step out when harm happens to all of us. There is power beyond what you can imagine in the margins, individually and collectively. The personal power tip is to act, however that looks for you, even when it means laying down your safety. Others will rise up, and the universe will have your back.

🔥 **Unleash your superhero**: Buy or create something connected to your superhero that you can wear. Maybe a T-shirt or socks. I have a Captain America shirt with the quote "I can do this all day." I also have Captain America socks that go to my knees. When

I wear these items in public, it captures attention and occasionally leads to positive comments. Wear the item and if you get a comment, create a one-line response. I say, "Captain America reminds me I can be a superhero too." You might be surprised by what responses follow. If you are not ready to respond, just wear it and embrace the empowered, positive feelings it can bring you. I wore my Captain America socks while writing this book!

🔥 **Manifestation affirmation:** My courage and my actions make a meaningful difference in my life and in the lives of those around me. When I take actions from a place of integrity and courage, in service of myself, in service of others, and in service of the greater good of humanity, it creates positive and meaningful impact in my life and in the world.

Assemble community for action

Find and build community

You have unleashed your superhero and ignited your personal power. You may be early on or far along your journey. You are showing up fully in who you are, and you are achieving the desires of your heart, but you want to do more about what is breaking your heart—more purposeful and mission-driven work individually and/or collectively with others. You want to make a difference in other people's lives—in the broader society.

It's time to assemble—assemble community for collective action. But before you can assemble, you have to find and build community. People coming together to support one another for a shared mission and collective action, igniting our personal power together, is creating community and movement, and building community is necessary for social change. Making a difference begins right where you are.

Find and build it in your home, in your workplace, in your community. You are enough. When you choose to activate your personal power and unleash your superhero, you also help activate it in others, whether or not your intention was to find and/or build community. Activating self-activates others. It will spread and expand like fire. It can build community, creating a circle of safety and support while activating collective power.

Your actions and who you are can create movement. Movement and change happen faster and is more sustainable when we effectively and collectively come together.

There is power in community for both individuals and for groups desiring positive and impactful social change in an unjust world.

I'm also going to tell you that finding community, however it looks, is essential to helping you consistently activate your own personal power and continuing your self-growth and betterment that you want as well as doing what you feel is right. Just think how much easier it is to disrupt those limiting voices and thoughts and move forward with successful execution when you surround yourself with a community of people on a similar path of self-awareness, growth, and purposeful actions. Remove or limit the energy and time you put into things and people who do not genuinely support your authentic self, purpose, and journey.

When it comes to finding or building a community that will actively take collective action, it may not seem easy, especially in such a divided world that also has competing priorities. There are extremists that will never change and dangerous people with dangerous agendas. But, let me remind you, there are also millions upon millions of people with primarily good intentions who are along a spectrum falling somewhere between the extremes on social issues that impact women, the LGBTQ+ community, and other marginalized groups.

They may lack knowledge and understanding, or they may not have a human connection to the issues, or they may lack direction on actions to take. What I see often is they don't see their own personal value and power in helping create impactful change. They don't see themselves as superheroes on the issues that impact us.

Valuing self and recognizing the power in self to make an impactful difference is the starting point to building community for meaningful collective action. We don't get far when there is not a human connection and people don't see their personal value and power in how they can make a difference. Starting there will help us ignite personal and collective power to successfully build a community of superheroes that will continue to expand and take collective action together to make a difference and drive social change in an unjust world.

Demonstrate genuine care for people

Hey, Superhero. You are enough, and you have the personal power in who you are to make a meaningful difference in your life and in the world. You must put yourself first to identify and unleash your personal power before you can then effectively serve others. One way to effectively serve others is to build a community of support.

You can find and build community with your actions. "How?" you may ask. We build connection and community by putting people first. What do I mean by that? Putting people first means grounding our decisions and actions in and leading from a place of genuine care. I believe many of us want to be better humans and we want to see all people and all living things on this Earth treated with genuine care and respect. If you deeply care about people and stay grounded in the value of putting people first through acts of genuine care, then community and collective action will happen much faster and will be more sustainable over time.

It starts like this: You must set aside all that you assume or believe about people and particular groups. For example, beliefs around their political party, their culture, their opinions, their expertise or lack thereof, their gender, their occupation, their age, their privilege, and their educational status. All the things that cause you to judge them and make assumptions about how they will respond to you.

It's important to recognize the biases that you have that may be preventing you or causing you to hesitate in choosing to engage another group or individual, particularly someone who might be quite different from yourself or might be more similar than you may have first thought. Judgments and biases limit us and make it much harder to build community. It makes it harder to recognize the superhero within someone else.

Demonstrating genuine care for people begins with recognizing people are first and foremost human, and every human life has value. It begins with judging less, listening more, and demonstrating empathy. Inviting them and creating space for them to share their story, their lived experience of who they are with you, what they care about and why. It opens the door to understanding another person's thoughts and feelings from their perspective and lived experience.

That action helps to break down barriers and invites connection and collaboration. They will be more responsive and open when you bring them to an issue you care about by first hearing what they care about and demonstrating empathy and genuine care for them as people first. Creating a safe space where they feel valued and seen will also help them to see their own value and the value in taking collective action with you.

Now, this is not always easy particularly for members of historically marginalized groups who have been harmed and have trauma connected to people, professions, institutions, and systems. They may not be able to do this in all circumstances and that's okay. That is why it is important for those who are able to go into difficult places and difficult conversations to lead the way for themselves and others.

I will also say if you take the approach I am recommending and the person or group does not respond in return with genuine care but with hate or harm, or even resistance and inauthenticity, do not invest any more energy into them. Put your energy into someone else. You can only offer genuine care and help to the end of your fingertips. If they don't accept, you shouldn't go any further. You can't force it and you will waste time and energy that can be used elsewhere. It's not about you. If they don't accept it, they are either not ready to receive it or don't plan on changing anytime soon. Remember, you don't need everyone on board for big, impactful change to occur. Invest in the people that just need that spark and connection to join forces with you.

Putting people first and demonstrating genuine care for others is one of my most important values, and I personally know how powerful it is building connection and community that leads to impactful, collective action. However, I have to also check myself at times. I'm only perfect in knowing I'm not perfect. We all have personal biases and beliefs that can prevent progress and collaboration, and we should regularly check in with ourselves.

Let me give you a practical workplace example. Legal teams and lawyers have really slowed me down at times, particularly when I have been focused on being proactive and innovative, leading big initiatives intended to reduce or eliminate harm that happens to people online or in real life. In fact, legal teams are routinely one of the most difficult teams to work with in trust and safety and social advocacy across tech and other industries because they are often overly risk averse and are heavily reactive instead of proactive. These teams can be huge blockers, creating barriers that feel impossible to overcome at times.

Early in my tech industry career as a leader, getting safety and sexual violence trainings, proactive education, visible campaigns, and even related language past the legal team felt like a continuous battle. Other team members and colleagues were regularly coming to me disappointed and frustrated saying, "I can't get this past legal, can you help?" And there was never just one attorney to deal with, there were many! You would think you were making progress and then it would get into the hands of the ligation team and go nowhere. They were often described as a thorn in everyone's side. Everything would come to a full stop. It felt like a war at times.

I realized I had to get the legal team on my team if I was going to be successful in making an impact, figuring out how to get them to work with us rather than against us. I planned on starting with the most difficult group within that team first—the litigation attorneys. I had to start with the people I honestly didn't really like at times, who had said things that

I felt were insensitive. I, like many, believed these attorneys cared more about the company than they did for people. I saw them as cold-hearted and uncaring.

Now, I'm sure that actually does fit the profile of some litigation attorneys in corporations, but I also know I was not being fair to those who were leading the litigation team, and other legal team members I was working with. I was allowing my own personal biases and beliefs about them to adversely impact my judgment and approach. I was making assumptions and judgments about people without making any effort to get to know them as people and better understand their responsibilities, challenges, and motivations. Here I was a leader who knew good and well the approach I should be taking; the approach I knew was the right thing to do, yet I was not taking my own advice or being true to the value I professed to have. It was time to make things right.

I started by putting myself in their shoes and began to feel compassion for them as people first. They were just doing a job they cared about, bringing their expertise and knowledge to support the organization they worked for. They probably never imagined that someday in their career they would be sitting across from a family who lost a child, or another woman just like them that had been brutally harmed, with the responsibility to provide a response and support to those people.

How could they ever know what that would feel like? Or what if it was tragically similar to something in their own lived experience? Hearing story after story from those harmed, and then trying to balance doing their job well with also showing care for people by searching for the right responses and the right support couldn't be easy. Even a single experience or a single story would not be easy for any human to endure. Hearing horrific stories that are sometimes hard to even begin to comprehend. Stories you may never forget. Stories of impact you may not be an expert in responding to.

I knew exactly what it felt like hearing stories of harm to human beings. I heard them over and over again as a police officer. I saw the stories up close in real time. People reporting and sitting in front of me telling me about their worst day—the worst moments of their lives. I knew personally how hard and heartbreaking it was to sit with a family who had just lost their child. I knew how hard it was to sit with a woman who had been sexually assaulted and now had to tell details of that story to me. Many of those stories I have never forgotten, and I carry them with me today. They remind me of my purpose and the difference I can make. They remind me I can be a public servant who shows genuine care and support for people no matter where I am.

We had scheduled training and a series of one-on-one meetings for the litigation team that I was personally presenting and engaging in. I decided to use the training and meetings as an opportunity to begin to engage the litigation attorneys in a different way. I decided to start the training with gratitude for them, recognizing their value, and I chose to demonstrate empathy by sharing with them how I could personally relate to the difficulty they faced in their jobs.

I shared parts of my personal experience that I knew they would be able to relate to. I wanted them to hear that I knew how hard it must be to do what they do. In addition, I shared how much value and positive impact I believed they could bring to the global epidemic of sexual violence that was so much bigger than the company we were all working for. I also offered them genuine support and extended an invitation to work together on a bigger mission.

On that day of the training there was an immediate shift of energy in the room and new and improved connections and relationships resulted. Several told me they felt seen and heard by me. Those conversations and many that followed opened the door to learning more and sharing more. The litigation attorneys were more open to collaboration with me and my team after that, and we worked through differences quicker and more easily together.

As a result, a deep connection formed, and a community expanded. We began to work more collaboratively on meaningful, collective actions, and over time some of them also recognized and found purpose in what broke their hearts. Many are still making a difference today with their voices and through meaningful actions, and they designed a legal approach to safety that is a model to learn from.

I still adore many of the attorneys I've worked with throughout my career. Particularly the ones who showed up with integrity, openness, and respect for people. One of them became the love of my life. I never saw that coming! Another one does a very good imitation of me, and there are still others who are some of my biggest cheerleaders. We created connections that will last a lifetime. I still continue to tease some of those attorneys about being cold-hearted lawyers, but it comes with a wink and a smile. Now, after building a shared connection and community through empathy and sharing my own personal experiences, I see them, and they see me.

Even though we first felt like adversaries, showing genuine care and empathy to these attorneys as people first, acknowledging and seeing their value, forming a human connection, and providing opportunity for action ignited meaningful, collective action in the community with one another.

It can happen with one, it can happen with twenty, it can happen with hundreds, it can happen with thousands, and it can happen with multitudes beyond your imagination. It is all movement, and it is all meaningful. I believe putting people first and demonstrating genuine care for others is crucial and necessary for successful and sustainable collective action and meaningful social change.

The power in a shared vision and narrative

You can't effectively build a community that will take collective action together without a shared vision and a narrative grounded in truth and integrity. You also have to share that vision and narrative out loud. When you talk about it, people who share and believe in that vision will begin to show up.

Just like you, people are often searching for something they can be a part of that is bigger than themselves and that is making a real difference in the world around us. They often feel helpless and overwhelmed by what is happening around them in an unjust world. They are looking for mission-driven opportunities and community. Opportunities to support and ways to be involved in positive social change. You could be that spark that helps bring it to life and ignites a fire within them.

When you identify what is breaking your heart then develop a vision statement that embodies it. Write down what you want to manifest connected to that vision. When you share a vision that people feel connected to, it will inspire them. It will begin to build a community, and it will bring you allies. Maybe you've already thought through what the vision and narrative is, including how you believe you get there. Start sharing it. Start building and people and pathways will begin to manifest and appear.

As you share, everyday superheroes will surface and will rally around a shared vision with you when you are coming from a place of integrity and genuine care for people. If they feel you genuinely care about them, they will also feel safe with you. Safe to take collective action. People may not know exactly what role they will play, but together you can help them recognize the value they bring to the mission and identify actions they can take. All movements, and people who have led movements, had a vision that people who followed them believed in it.

Visions not only inspire us, but they give us a sense of belonging and focus. They provide direction and help us plan our mission and our next steps. At each point along the journey, they remind us of purpose and give us pride in service to the greater good of all. They bring connection and people together to begin to architect and manifest something beautiful and impactful that gives life meaning together in community.

When you share your vision, when you share what is breaking your heart, when you create an intellectually rigorous and substantive narrative that embodies it and demonstrate genuine care, like-minded everyday superheroes will appear. People you never expected will show up and help you. You will also find others with a shared vision who may already be making progress on it, and you can join forces.

Weave it into your story. Share it in your workplace. Share it with loved ones and those in your community. Share it with those you engage with regularly. Leverage your connections. They may bring additional people, knowledge, and skills and may want to be a part of supporting you or helping create the next steps with you.

We frequently assume that people are just too busy with their work, with their families, and their own lives. We don't want to bother them. We tell ourselves we don't want to take their time. Or we believe they just don't care because we don't see them taking proactive or reactive action. We don't recognize that those people may be searching for that opportunity or moment to rise up and embrace purpose collectively with you.

We all have time. We all choose what we put our time and energy into. People often want to be able to say that they've done something purposeful in their life that made a difference in their own life and in the lives of others. They also want to be able to tell the story of how they were able to make a meaningful difference. They may be just waiting for somebody like you to show up so they can show up too.

Let me also tell you that not everyone will join you. That's okay. You don't need everyone to activate collective power to create impactful change in an unjust world. I remember distinctly when I walked through the door at 1455, what we called the Uber corporate office in San Francisco. I walked in there in 2016 thinking, "Wow, if I can just get everyone to care about preventing and disrupting violence against women and other vulnerable groups as much as I do, look at the big change we can make—look at the scale of impact we can make."

I was hired at Uber in 2016 to help them talk about and appropriately address the safety issues and harm that was happening connected to their platform, both reactively and proactively. The focus would be all safety, but a specific focus on sexual and gender-based violence was needed. My nickname in policing was Tornado. That probably gives you a little bit of an idea about what happened when I walked in the door at Uber! Let's just say they brought in the right expert, and I'm grateful there were leaders there that genuinely cared about these issues, saw the need for someone like me, and supported my work.

I learned early on along my journey in policing and again in tech that I would never convince every single person to care about the safety of women and marginalized groups as much as we deserved. For one, it is a personal journey and lived experience that not everyone understands. I had to start from a place of empathy and shift to trying to understand the people I was engaging with and how they operated and what they cared about.

The majority of decision-makers and leaders throughout my career didn't look like me. They didn't have similar experiences. They didn't come from the community I'm a part of. In fact, more times than not, I found myself in a room talking to decision-makers, who were mostly men, about how to create safety for women and the most marginalized. I should have gotten hazard pay for that!

Then there are those that deeply care and get it, and they show up just when you need them rather than walking away. I found lots of superheroes at Uber that included men, women and non-binary people. In my early days working there, while partnering with police and hearing from customer service agents, I became aware of trends around human trafficking connected to the platform. Traffickers use all forms of public and private forms of transportation to transport their victims to locations. It was no surprise to hear they were also using rideshare. Drivers were reporting suspicious activity to customer service but were for the most part unsure of what was actually happening at times due to a lack of education and understanding on both sides.

Utilizing my own expertise and my connections in law enforcement, I started creating an initiative to address it. I was determined to disrupt it. One component of that initiative was to develop specialized education for drivers to help them know how to identify when trafficking was likely occurring and to then know what steps to take to report it. To do it right would take getting several cross-functional teams and executive leadership on board.

It meant creating messaging and getting it in front of drivers using all communication means we had access to such as in-app, email, and in greenlight hubs used for onboarding drivers. It also meant developing training for customer service agents. And that was just the education component. There was a lot more that needed to be done including working closely with police and national and international expert groups on the right solutions.

I started using my voice and sharing the narrative and vision with everyone I encountered on the inside to try to get support. People started showing up when I chose to share the vision out loud. Someone in the organization heard me and connected me with an everyday superhero named Gabe. Gabe was a marketing manager for the southwest region and had the distinction of being the first employee hired by Uber in the Phoenix office. He was also the first person to join forces with me. Gabe wasn't just a marketing manager—he was a marketing genius and created beauty and magic with everything he touched. He also cared deeply about people and particularly the issue of human trafficking and had been trying to educate drivers in his region.

We started brainstorming on how we could work together to disrupt it, get leadership on board, and create a much larger initiative across all regions Uber operated in. Getting budget and funding was not at all easy for big initiatives like this, and it took lots of hard work, lots of conversations, and lots of time. We had to get scrappy in the beginning, as we were not successful in obtaining a budget for education at the start—but we were not about to give up. I continued to talk to national and local law enforcement and work with our teams while also having discussions with leaders. A pivotal breakthrough occurred when Gabe was able to get us a meeting with Cindy McCain at her home in Phoenix, Arizona.

Cindy McCain is a champion for human rights and is currently a United States Ambassador to the United Nations Agencies for Food and Agriculture in Rome and the Executive Director of the World Food Programme (WFP). Along with the McCain Institute, Cindy has been an advocate and leader in combating human trafficking.

I distinctly remember sitting down with her explaining the totality of the unique circumstances that we were facing and discussing what was needed, while also sharing that we were unable to get any budget to create specialized education at this time. We had some unique needs, and we needed a leader and organization to help us, essentially for free.

She looked me in the eye and said, "Yes!" enthusiastically without hesitation. "I, along with the McCain Institute, will help you create the education and tips needed. Let me know what else I can do to help get the support you need." The McCain Institute was the first organization to agree to partner with us to help create Uber's first specialized tips and education for drivers, and Cindy continued to be a supporter of our efforts. I am deeply grateful to her because at that time no other individual or organization I had reached out to was willing to do what she did. Those actions would later open the door to more partnerships and eventually budget and funding for our initiative and for the organizations working to disrupt human trafficking.

With Cindy and the McCain Institute commitment to help us, it was now time for us to work on the educational initiative for drivers. I got leadership approval, and Gabe started working his magic on the creative content for things like the web page and driver communications. We also got a local general manager and ally to provide us with some funding for an educational video.

Gabe created Uber's first human trafficking prevention video, with the help of a personal connection and friend of his who shot the video for little cost. I'll never forget that Gabe also helped me create my first executive deck and presentation pitching the need for education regarding human trafficking. It meant so much to me that he helped me every step of the way.

I was a cop that came to Uber, and it was very early days in my career in tech. I had the topic expertise and the language to build the case, but I didn't have a background in the tech environment and had no idea how to create the type of business case and presentation deck that would capture the buy-in and meet the expectations of executive leaders. Gabe not only had the marketing expertise, but he also knew the rideshare business and operations as well as any leader. He created an executive deck for me that was visually powerful and impactful that stopped people in their tracks. He had my back every step of the way.

That was just one of many steps. This story has many more unforgettable chapters to share another day. Ultimately, I got the corporate funding and leadership approval and support for the broader educational initiative, public campaign and partnerships, and an executive sponsor that made it a priority. It wasn't long before our small southwest educational initiative turned into a U.S.-wide initiative and campaign reaching 750K drivers and eventually went international starting in Latin America. Superheroes from teams all over Uber joined us, together creating a movement and taking the initiative to new heights. Year after year, the initiative continued to expand. It is still happening today. Most importantly, drivers were given tools to help disrupt human trafficking and they did. Many became unexpected, everyday superheroes.

Gabe created a powerful, impactful video and creative content for our human trafficking educational tips that brought them visually to life, and he was instrumental with me in the operational execution of the initiative across all regions. What we accomplished with the positive and impactful success of that first initiative to combat human trafficking was vital to opening the door to more conversations and creating pathways to much bigger safety-related initiatives to support the safety of women, the LGBTQ+ community, and other marginalized groups.

When you use your voice to share what is breaking your heart, along with a vision and a narrative from a place of truth and integrity that won't let you go unheard, I promise you everyday superheroes will rise up to meet you and join forces. They will show up, and together you can collectively create magic and movements while building community.

I am deeply grateful for the superheroes, like Gabe, who rose up with me and continue to rise up every day for others.

Leverage expert partners

Sometimes you will need additional backup from a community of superheroes to help you successfully accomplish mission-driven work and drive impactful change in what is breaking your heart and the hearts of others, particularly when you identify it working within systems and organizations such as corporations.

Anytime you need additional help creating safe spaces, addressing harm happening to a group, creating impactful initiatives, and even help creating grassroots movements, you can always call on additional backup to help you build community, accelerate execution, and create the spaces that women, the LGBTQ+ community, and other historically marginalized groups deserve. That help and collective power can come from leveraging local community, national and international experts, third-party groups, and NGOs. Leaders, organizations, and institutions don't know everything, and they shouldn't pretend that they do. That's where thought-leading expert groups can help. They understand our cultural and unique lived experiences and the needs of groups and have the expertise to back it up.

There are third-party experts and NGOs around the world that have a primary focus on women, the LGBTQ+ community, and other marginalized groups. Some are frontline workers that provide direct services that are working with specific communities, engaging with them daily, and making sure they are seen and heard. Others are focused on government, policy, and regulations. Some are focused on prevention and education. They understand current lived experiences, the current state of laws and regulations, and they know the history.

They are investing in understanding and awareness and work in the space of prevention. They prevent harm against communities, disrupt harm as it occurs, and respond with education and understanding in their communities and organizations across the world. They make certain that communities are being supported appropriately and they work to create the right policies needed. They work every single day on the front lines for the most marginalized groups and communities in need.

Leveraging additional expert partners and groups, once you identify a specific need or cause, can help you get approval, build or bolster a business case, and help you and others develop the right programs, initiatives, and support. They can also help you bolster and build a business case for the change that needs to occur and the improvements that need to be made that benefit people, community, and the business. You can also help them. You can amplify their reach and bring groups together in collaboration that don't traditionally work together.

I've leveraged my expert partners and colleagues throughout my career since first engaging with NGOs and advocacy groups early on in law enforcement. When I entered tech, I brought not only my lived experience and safety expertise, but I also brought a community collaborative and collective approach with me into an industry that was not good at proactively engaging and thoughtfully partnering with safety and inclusion leaders and groups in the communities they were operating in, as well as with third-party expert groups that were serving marginalized groups in those communities. Building deep and impactful relationships begins by inviting them in and listening and learning from them, and then meaningfully partnering with them on initiatives that support and create positive change for both employees and consumers.

In corporations, my teams and I leveraged expert groups creating global partnerships and initiatives. To give you an idea of what type of groups I'm referring to, here are examples of some of these expert groups in the U.S.: NO MORE, me too. Movement, Raliance, Callisto, Human Rights Campaign (HRC), The Trevor Project, The Anti-Violence Project, Ujima, Polaris, Esperanza United, and A Call to Men. There are many other national and international organizations in these spaces you can find in the resource section of this book that may be helpful to you.

Keep in mind that there are large international and national organizations, but there are also local community-based organizations that are waiting and willing to help you that desperately need support. Local and state coalitions are great to work with. One of my favorite local organizations in my home state of Arizona to support is one in ten, an organization that creates safe spaces and support for LGBTQ+

youth throughout my local community and state. Some of the best organizations you can support for the LGBTQ+ community are organizations supporting young people and creating safety and inclusion for them. It's one thing I wish I could have had as a Queer kid and creating a safer world for our future leaders and changemakers is worth our investment.

Working directly with experts helps us achieve individual and collective mission-driven work within organizations and in our communities, and it sends a message of genuine care and support to women, the LGBTQ+ community, and other marginalized groups, addressing our specific and unique needs around physical, emotional, and psychological safety.

When you go looking to find or build a community, one place you can find it is in experts with lived experience, directly supporting communities. Leveraging them not only brings expertise and collective power, but it also multiples that power and those voices exponentially by including the power and voices of the people they represent and serve. Together, we become a larger group with a shared vision of creating a safe and respectful world for everyone.

Elevate others

In my experience, another essential way to build community and ignite people to take collective action together to make a difference is to elevate and empower others so they can use their personal power. People want to be a part of something they can also have ownership in, and you can give them that.

You have to start first by putting your ego on the shelf. Yes, I said your ego. Put it on the shelf and leave it there. When you elevate others, you yourself will also elevate. Don't worry about it. When you invest in other people, it will not only come back to you, but you will also help unleash more superheroes. If you become selfish and very siloed in your work and don't give others ownership, people won't stay for long and getting them to take collective action will be very difficult.

Inspire them. Empower them. Give them ownership. Mutual ownership creates a space where they feel the vision is also their vision—a shared vision. Elevate them through service and through collaboration. Allow them to bring their shared ideas. When people connect personally, and they have ownership in something, they're going to feel far more safe, motivated, and inspired to work toward the vision and a mission. They will feel like they belong to a community. Elevating and empowering others is crucial and essential to assembling a larger community and movement that will take successful collective action.

Visions are meant to be shared. If you give people ownership, they will continue to work at it, they will continue to prioritize it, and they will continue to find ways to achieve the vision and the mission-driven work that drives change. You want to create owners, not just followers. Operating from a place of service, creating shared ownership, sharing the successes and sharing the failures, will inspire innovation and ideas. We are more motivated and inspired when we know that what we have ownership in is making a difference in both our lives and the lives of others.

Now, along the way, sharing visions, sharing what breaks your heart, and sharing ideas with people will also attract people with selfish intent. People are going to show up who don't have good intent and have selfish reasons for helping. They may take your ideas, make them their own, take credit for them, and go forward in a direction you may not have envisioned. It doesn't feel good when you are deceived by someone you trusted, invested in, or helped, and they use you and your ideas for their own personal gain.

I will tell you this. Let it go and let them go. Don't take it personally. Just keep doing the work and following your intuition and the currents of your heart. Keep sharing the vision. It just means that you had a really good idea, a vision that created impact, you achieved success and it led to individual and collective action. More times than not, they also come back needing help with execution. And people will also know and be able to find the truth. Truth will prevail, and the universe will have your back.

If someone is also being purely selfish and not acting with integrity, disconnect from them. When you are focused on doing the right thing from a place of genuine care, the universe will keep revealing to you people, ideas, and opportunities to create change and movement. If you are igniting meaningful action, you are doing something right.

Elevating others builds community and ignites people to take collective action together creating meaningful change. The majority of people you help elevate will keep moving forward with you and others toward a shared vision, expanding and reaching heights beyond your imagination.

Chapter 7 activators

Reflection questions:

➧ Have I found or built a community that values its individual power and leverages collective power to create impactful change? Is it connected to what breaks my heart? Are the actions grounded in truth and integrity? If I haven't found it, what will be my next steps to finding it or building it myself?

➧ How am I demonstrating genuine care for people in my home, in the workplace, and in other places where I am? What personal biases may be preventing me from showing genuine care to someone? What are two or three ways I can demonstrate genuine care for someone who I would describe as difficult, uncaring, ignorant or maybe just complacent, about one thing or many things I care about? It could be more than one person and one or more than one of the descriptors could describe them.

🔥 **Personal power tip**: Use your personal power to demonstrate genuine care, elevate and empower others, both individuals and groups. It is one of the quickest paths to successful and sustainable collective action. Inspire people. Give them ownership. Mutual ownership creates a space where others feel your vision; "the vision" is also their vision, a shared vision. You can be a public servant from anywhere. Elevate people and other groups through genuine care, service, and through collaboration. Allow them to bring their shared ideas. When people connect personally, and they have a level of ownership, they're going to be far more motivated and inspired to work toward a vision and mission. They will feel like they belong to a community. Demonstrating genuine care and elevating and empowering others are some of the quickest and most important actions to assembling a larger community and movement that will take collective action.

🔥 **Unleash your superhero**: Share the superhero you have chosen with others who are not that personally close to you. Maybe it's a colleague or a team member of a team you are leading. Tell them who it is, your favorite quote by the superhero, and why you relate and connect to that specific superhero. Ask them what superhero character they most connect with.

🔥 **Manifestation affirmation**: I show genuine care for people and help activate other superheroes. Our collective actions drive impactful social change. I surround myself with a community of people who help me grow and who support and encourage me to achieve the desires of my heart while also making a difference in the world.

Collective activation: Move forward with boldness and disruption

Take a stand... and don't stop there!

All right superhero. Yes, I'm talking to you. Go ahead and embrace it and say, "Yes, I am a superhero!" Are you ready to activate and lead groups of superheroes? Or maybe you're ready to be a part of using your personal power for something bigger than yourself, becoming part of a group of superheroes that makes a big, bold, disruptive, positive difference in the world around you? Do you see yourself saying, "I had a role in that positive change that happened, and it feels amazing. Let's do it again and again!"?

If you want to activate or be a part of a community activation to take collective action and ignite movements, you must be willing to take a stand. Stand up for what's right. And not just once. You must take a public stand over and over again and do it consistently with actions to back it up. It makes it come to life and it makes it real. It results in real, sustainable change.

People are more likely to follow and believe those who consistently and authentically show up in both word and action. It also inspires and empowers others to do the same. Whether it's in the workplace, or your community, or personally, you have to be willing to take a stand no matter the place, no matter the circumstances, with family, friends, and others you engage with for big, bold change to occur. You have to take a stand when it's difficult. When it is uncomfortable. You have to be willing to have difficult conversations if you want individual and collective change to occur. Become comfortable with the uncomfortable.

You might ask, "What is the difference between using your voice and taking a stand?" Taking a stand is more than words. It is actions and values that are consistent with your words. It means you walk the talk, especially when it gets tough. You want your reputation to be such that when people talk about you, they say you stand for what's right, no matter the situation, no matter the circumstance, no matter how challenging. They will feel safe and confident in a community with you because others are more likely to embrace collective action when both leaders and followers are authentic and consistent in standing for what is right.

You also must take a stand during what I call windows of opportunity. A window of opportunity occurs when what you stand for, when what breaks your heart, becomes a topic of conversation or even conflict in your own circles or even broader in the world. I leveraged windows of opportunity often in the corporate setting. It may be a moment of heightened attention that you can capitalize on when something has caused people to pause and evaluate their own beliefs, actions, and role.

This can be a moment in time for starting, continuing, or amplifying a message or movement because people are observing and listening. It becomes a window of opportunity to remove wrong perceptions, erroneous beliefs, expand perspectives, and ignite people to embrace a vision, recognizing their own personal power and role while igniting collective action. It is a moment to strike—to strike that match that can ignite a fire of movement and change that spreads far and wide.

For me, Tarana Burke and the #MeToo movement is a great example of this. In 2006, survivor and activist Tarana Burke founded the #MeToo movement. For years she took a consistent stand over and over again, bringing resources and support for survivors of sexual violence where none had existed before. She brought healing and awareness to the disparate impact of sexual violence on Black women, Indigenous women, LGBTQ+ people, people with disabilities, and all communities of color.

A window of opportunity happened in 2017 when #MeToo went viral. Millions of people around the globe took a stand and courageously shared parts of their personal stories of sexual violence and harassment. There were 12 million comments, responses, and stories shared on social media alone in 24 hours. #MeToo quickly became a global movement. It created a moment of heightened awareness as the world's attention was captured. Tarana and others seized the moment, their window of opportunity, to take a stand in solidarity and then backed it up with actions. The moment created visibility and awareness like never before related to the sexual harassment and sexual violence epidemic and created a community for those impacted. That window of opportunity ignited people in a movement toward sustainable, positive change.

Tarana has said, "The world is forever changed because of #MeToo. The language we use is shifting, replacing words like victim with survivor. We talk about mental health and healing, and employers are crafting thoughtful human resource policies, not just reacting after a workplace harassment crisis. Consumers are more conscientious about the cultural content they consume and vocal about calling out rape culture when they see it."[1]

The impact of this movement went far beyond simple visibility. And although Tarana may have been cast into the international spotlight when #MeToo went viral, what we found when digging deeper was a woman who didn't take a stand at just that one moment in time. She had always taken a stand, over and over again starting in 2006, being visible and vocal where she could, and then backed up her talk with real, genuine actions. That is a very important reason why the movement she started in 2006 went viral in 2017 and continues to grow and make a bold, meaningful impact today.

She continues to serve historically marginalized groups and helps them along their unique healing journey, and she also continues to build a community of superheroes that are tirelessly working collectively to disrupt sexual violence wherever it happens. Tarana said something profound that inspires me. She tells us that the spaces where harm happens are also the spaces where healing has to happen. She says that movement work is about healing work—and not just individual healing but healing a community.[1]

Igniting your personal power so that you can take a stand in response to something that breaks your heart or someone else's heart and then backing it up with consistent and authentic actions unleashes other superheroes, builds community, activates collective action, creates movements, and perhaps most importantly, heals community. Tarana and her community of superheroes are helping to heal our world. You can too.

Are you consistently taking a stand and then backing that up with action when those moments and windows of opportunity present themselves? That's what creates the big, bold, disruptive, and sustainable change the world needs.

It's time to take a stand… and don't stop there. Superheroes keep making it happen.

Activating collective power to drive bold and disruptive change

We need big and disruptive social change because harm continues to happen. WE are women, members of the LGBTQ+ community, the Black community, the Indigenous community, all people of color, people with disabilities, and other historically marginalized groups. There is power in the margin. We must lead the change we want to see. The change the world needs.

We can create safe and empowering spaces to activate individual and collective action to drive bold and disruptive change. Creating safe and empowering spaces allows us and others to see and recognize our personal power and unleash the superhero within each of us. We must work through our own fear and disrupt the limiting voices and thoughts that we hear so often and that the systems and communities we are a part of so often reinforce. Creating safe and empowering spaces gives people permission to use their voices to change the conversation—to change the narrative. Creating safe and empowering spaces helps to ignite people's personal power and creates community to assemble for collective action.

It takes bold and often disruptive actions to create safe and empowering spaces to drive impactful social change. It happens through the disruption of beliefs and systems that cause harm to others and the institutions that support them, and through disruption in your own personal life, leading you to find pathways to your own healing, freedom, purpose, and power.

I believe that disruption in these spaces activates transformational impact individually and across society. In your home, in your communities, and on the inside and outside of organizations you can inspire and activate toward the big, bold change that you want to see in yourself and in the world.

Disruption of self and the beliefs and systems that surround us is not easy, and often requires us to lay down our safety. It begins when we believe we are enough and give ourselves permission to take that first step into our personal truth and power. But it can't stop there. We must keep believing and keep taking those steps.

People will only gather together to take bold and disruptive action collectively when they embrace their full self, their personal power, when they don't feel alone, and when they feel like a genuine community will have their backs. Or, they have gotten to the point where they are so angry, so broken, so tired of giving in, so tired of being harmed, so tired of watching others being harmed, that they lay their safety and fear down and move into personal power and bold, disruptive action.

Are we going to wait until each one of us is tired, angry, and broken? Are we going to keep waiting for those who have oppressed us to finally decide to see and hear us?

I won't wait.

Women and historically marginalized groups have a critical role to play in social activism. We need bold and disruptive change, and it is up to us to lead the way. We must take the lead on creating safe and empowering spaces for ourselves and others. No one else is going to create these for us in the way that we deserve.

We must first and foremost invest in ourselves and then others, across our communities, helping individuals see their own value and personal power, creating safety and unleashing superheroes along the way. How much longer are we going to walk past each other in the intersections, tired and frustrated, fighting similar battles? We have become too siloed, complacent, silenced, and paralyzed by fear.

We can make more big, bold, sweeping changes when we come together collectively. We are more connected and similar than we think. Along my journey, I have interacted with and worked with various members of historically marginalized groups across the world. What I too frequently see across my community and other marginalized groups are people who don't feel safe, who feel stuck, who feel helpless, and who struggle greatly in recognizing and embracing their own value and personal power.

I can help you identify bold actions to take in your workplace, in your community, in your everyday life. I can tell you about the actions, strategies, and practices I've used that have been successful. I can share what others have accomplished. I can tell you how to take legislative action. I can tell you how to leverage other superheroes and representation in organizations. I can tell you how to use your consumer power, and how to use social and other platforms effectively. I can help you identify how to take a stand for what is right. Together, we can put our energy and power into where we can make the most impact collectively.

But it won't be effective in creating the meaningful, sustainable change we need unless you first start with self. You must appropriately and continually address your own woundedness, and the impact of rejection on your self-view. You must work to disrupt the limiting thoughts and beliefs, grow and continue to expand in self-awareness and authenticity. I know it's not always going to be easy, but don't give up. You will get stronger and better.

You will reach a pivotal point where your power and ability to create change is undeniable. Those who have historically misused their power and control to harm you, others, and those who came before you, don't want you to reach this pivotal point. They will attempt to keep you in the margin and will continue to use the same narrative that they have been using—the narrative in our history that we didn't deserve. They will take actions to stop you and remind you that you don't have the power, alone or collectively, and you are not enough to create change. It's so woven into our history that there are even good people with good intentions who continue to support a narrative that advances the harm. It's where many of us get stuck, move slowly, or go no further.

It is our most important work leading to that pivotal moment. That pivotal moment, and moments thereafter, when we recognize and embrace our personal power and unleash the superhero within us—when I am enough to create change becomes our daily mantra. It will feel like fire engulfing and spreading through every cell of your body. So powerful, it spreads quickly and activates others. It is in those pivotal moments where history changes, where we take our power back and restore balance in society. It's how we activate and assemble to drive bold, disruptive, social change collectively.

This is also that moment when all those limiting voices and beliefs inside of us from the outside are the loudest, trying to stop this expansion into our personal power from happening. It's the moment that all those who have misused power and caused harm want to disrupt. Why? Because once that moment happens for us, we become unstoppable.

The personal power is within you, and you can help unleash that power in other women and members of historically marginalized groups. You have the power within you to create safe and empowering spaces for all of us to activate and rise up. It is the way to fully become who you are, achieve the desires of your heart, make an impactful difference in the world, and help build a community for collective action.

How are you doing this with the people you encounter and the places and systems you move through every day? Are you uncomfortable with the idea of disruption, yet you want to see it happen? Sometimes when I use the word disruption, it makes people feel uncomfortable. It shouldn't. Disruption is defined as "a break or interruption in the normal course or continuation of an activity or process."I don't know about you, but I don't want to remain on the same course we have historically been on, and it's going to take disruption to create better humans and a better world. That disruption begins with you.

We all need support. Find a community. Don't be afraid to ask for help. Find a life coach. Find a fellow disruptor, a fellow superhero. Leverage our increased representation across organizations, leverage your allies, and leverage the superheroes that came before you.

If you are reading this and you have knowledge and understanding of the issues, you are a member of the communities I referenced. You understand the impactful actions you can take, you recognize your value, and you have embraced your personal power—you must take the lead because you are able to do it and we need you. It will inspire and empower others to follow. It will rally others in the community to start movements where they are at. Others will join you.

Whatever you do professionally or personally, wherever you find yourself, whatever platform you have access to in order to connect and reach others, whether it is music, art, speaking, or providing a service, don't be afraid to find ways to use your personal power and weave the message of your heart into your work.

When you create safety for yourself, you can then create safety for others. When you use your personal power, you help activate and assemble other superheroes. When you create individual movements, you help ignite the opportunity for bigger movements. You can drive together with other leaders, leveraging collective power. Will you lay down your safety for yourself and others?

Stand in a place of hope

I recognize that it's hard. I recognize that it can be overwhelming and heavy at times. I recognize it isn't always fair. Listen, I get it too. As a Queer woman, I totally get it. It's hard to believe that things can change some days or that I am enough to make a dent in it. Some days I just want to quit. I want to escape from it all. Sometimes the reality is hard to sit with. It's been a tough journey for so many.

Add to it the increasing divisiveness, violence, and harm, challenges on and losses of our fundamental rights and the Covid-19 pandemic to top it off, it seems like it hasn't let up. People are tired, they're exhausted. They're seeking connection, community, and something meaningful. I believe they always have been. It's so important to encircle ourselves with people who support us, who believe in us, and who remind us day in and day out who we truly are, and the power we have to make a difference. Let me remind you that you are a superhero. Find more people to remind you.

I've leveraged friends, connections, coaches, counselors, and other superheroes, and let me remind you again that you should never be ashamed to ask for help and surround yourself with support. We need it to keep doing our personal development work. I call it our personal power work. Even superheroes are just human at the core. Women and members of historically marginalized communities face steeper challenges and steeper barriers. It's hard to maintain hope and so many people understandably have lost hope.

What I'm going to ask you to do, despite all that's going on around you, past and present, despite how grim it may seem at times, how overwhelming at times it may feel, how it may feel like it's not going to get any better, is to rise up. I need you—the world needs you—to rise up. Rise up and stand with me and others in a place of hope.

Let me help you understand what I mean by sharing this final story with you. One night while working as a law enforcement officer, I got a domestic violence call. Domestic violence calls are one of the most frequent calls police respond to and also one of the most dangerous types of calls. They are a daily occurrence across the world.

The night this call came, I responded and took the lead on the call. A woman had frantically called the emergency line letting law enforcement dispatchers know that her ex-boyfriend had showed up at her apartment with a gun. He had a history of violence, and he was not supposed to be in possession of any weapons. She said her ex-boyfriend had found out she had a new boyfriend, and he had showed up at her apartment threatening to kill the new boyfriend. The ex-boyfriend was currently outside the apartment. This call required an emergency response with lights and sirens because people and the public were in immediate danger. Several officers responded and joined me as my backup.

When we got to the apartment complex we couldn't get through the front gate because the code that we were given was not working. There was no time to waste, so we got out of our cars and proceeded on foot through a pedestrian entrance. I led the officers into the complex, and they provided me with cover.

Law enforcement dispatchers continued talking to us over our handheld radios, and they let us know that the ex-boyfriend had left the apartment and was now somewhere in the grounds of the apartment complex. They gave us a physical description of him including what he was wearing. They also indicated that a girlfriend of the woman, who lived in the same complex, and the new boyfriend were also somewhere in the complex attempting to calm and convince the ex-boyfriend to leave and not harm anyone.

As we walked through the complex, we found the apartment of the woman who had initially called police. A couple of officers broke off to her apartment to make contact and check on her welfare as we walked by. As I led the other officers forward into the complex, I looked down through the parking lot. I saw a woman and a man standing near a row of cars with another man who matched the description of the ex-boyfriend; the suspect we were looking for.

As I began to notify the other officers that I believed I had eyes on the suspect, he turned his head and spotted us. As soon as he made eye contact with us he pulled out a gun and started firing the gun in our direction. We were standing out in the open directly in his line of fire. For our protection, we immediately took cover behind anything we could get behind, even the street curb. Thankfully, no officers were hit by the gunfire.

After finding cover and cautiously standing back up, we looked down at the row of cars in the parking lot, but we couldn't see anybody. I then led the officers forward and we began to tactically clear each car for our safety, making our way carefully around and through the row of cars.

As we came around the back of one car, I saw the suspect. He was lying on the ground on his stomach with his arms out and his hand next to his gun. We would later find out that after firing off several rounds one of the bullets became lodged inside the gun and it would no longer work. He decided to give up and not flee. Lying next to the ex-boyfriend were the man and women we had seen with him. Both had been shot by the suspect and were lying in a pool of blood. The man who was believed to be the new boyfriend of the survivor/victim was already deceased. The woman, who was the girlfriend of the survivor/victim, who had been trying to calm the suspect and get him to leave, had been shot in the back of the head near her neck. She was still alive but losing lots of blood.

One of my backup officers took the suspect immediately into custody and took possession of the weapon, and I began performing emergency first aid to the woman who was still clinging to life until paramedics could arrive. She was bleeding heavily and going in and out of consciousness. With one hand, I covered the back of her neck to try to slow the bleeding coming from the gunshot wound. I took her other hand, and I placed it up against my bullet-proof outer vest over my heart and held it.

I talked to her in an attempt to keep her awake and conscious. "My name is Officer Tracey Breeden," I told her. "I am here with you, and I am giving you all my energy and strength. I want you to talk to me and try to stay with me." As I looked into her eyes, cradling her head, I told her, "Focus on living, just breathe and keep talking to me. I'm here with you, and I'm not leaving you." She was frightened, had difficulty speaking, and kept repeating that the ex-boyfriend had a gun. I reassured her that everyone was safe now.

"What's your name? Where do you live?" She told me her name, and then told me she had two young daughters that were in the apartment right across from where we were in the same complex. She communicated she felt safe with me as a woman officer and said, "I want you... I want a woman to tell my girls."

She continued to struggle to speak. "What do you want me to tell your girls?" I asked. "If I die, please, I want you to tell my girls," she responded. She kept telling me she thought she was going to die, and I could see that she was losing hope quickly. I promised her I would honor her wishes and I would be the one to tell her girls, but right now, I needed her to stay in a place of hope with me and stay focused on living.

"I'm not going to stop believing for you," I told her. "I need you to believe with me even though you may feel hopeless right now." I told her I was not going to let go of hope for her.

When all seems hopeless, when it seems like nothing's ever going to change, there are those of us who are able to continue to believe. Those of us who are able to continue to fight for others. Those of us who are able to continue to rise up and stand in a place of hope when others around us have lost hope.

I need you to stand in a place of hope with me. To continue to rise up and to stand with me believing that things can and will change. That things can get better. That humans can be better. That together we can collectively drive social change and create a better world. The world and our communities need those of us who are able to grasp and hold on to hope when it seems hopeless around us. When all hope seems lost. That can be you.

The woman who thought she was sure to die... lived. I never had to tell her daughters that they lost their mother to harm and violence. I'm standing in a place of hope that we will be able to tell all our children, young and old alike, that individuals, that groups across all intersections came together and drove meaningful, disruptive change. That we changed the systems. That we changed the institutions for the better. That we took back what was taken from us. That we created safe spaces not only for ourselves, but for those who needed them the most.

I'm still standing in that place of hope. Stand with me and let's disrupt together. You're already a superhero. See it. Be it. Help others see that they're superheroes too and together we will take big, bold actions.

People think I saved that woman's life that night, but what I tell them is I gave her hope, which gave her the power to save her own life. Who can you give hope to today? Have you become complacent? Rise up with me and let's stand together in a place of hope while taking action, while continuing to disrupt. Let's give one another our collective power.

I believe in you. I know you can do this. Don't lose hope. I got you. We got you. Your backup is all around you. You are not alone.

Women, members of the LGBTQ+ community, the Black community, the Indigenous community, all people of color, people with disabilities, and other historically marginalized groups. You know who you are. We hold the power, super-hero power, to drive social change through individual and collective action.

Harm continues to happen. Social change is needed.

You are more than enough to create change.

Begin with self and then...

assemble.

Chapter 8 activators

🕯 Reflection questions:

➤ How am I consistently and authentically taking a stand regarding what is breaking my heart? How am I showing up in both word and action? How can I play a critical role in social activism?

➤ How am I creating safe and empowering spaces, helping people recognize their personal power and ignite the superhero within them? How am I creating a community to assemble for collective action?

🔥 **Personal power tip**: Look out for windows of opportunity and moments to strike the match to make a move and light a fire of movement. The timing can be instrumental to successfully use your personal power. A window of opportunity occurs when what you stand for, what breaks your heart, becomes a topic of conversation or even conflict in your own circles, or even broader in the world. I leveraged windows of opportunity often in the corporate setting. It may be a moment of heightened attention that you can capitalize on when something has caused people to pause and evaluate their own beliefs and role. This can be a moment in time for starting, continuing, or amplifying a message or movement because people are observing and listening. It becomes a window of opportunity to remove wrong perceptions, erroneous beliefs, expand perspectives, and ignite people to embrace a vision, recognizing their own personal power and role while igniting collective action.

🔥 **Unleash your superhero**: It's time to embrace and weave your superhero character into your communications and engagements. Find fun and inspiring ways to use it to not only encourage yourself but to motivate and activate other superheroes. Watch the magic it creates as people begin to believe and unleash their own superhero within.

🔥 **Manifestation affirmation**: I am standing in a place of hope for myself and others. I have the personal power and superhero within me to create safe and empowering spaces for all of us to activate and rise up, creating social change.

Acknowledgments

Thank you to my community, my family, my friends, and every single person who has genuinely supported and encouraged me along my journey. I adore you all, and I'm deeply grateful for each of you.

Thank you to all the members of my teams over the years as well as those who "unofficially" joined me. You are super-heroes and always will be a part of my team and superhero family.

I want to give a special shout out to Michelle, Ginger, LiAnn, Renita, Carla, Jessica, Calen, Nan, Johnathon, Mindy, Dianni, Pam, Jane, Robbie, Carolyn and my sparkle sisters Rachel and Carley, along with the Practical Inspiration team who helped me with the creation of this book by providing feedback, insightful guidance, and words of validation and encouragement.

Thank you to my life coach, mentor, and superhero Flyn, who helped me find the power within me to recognize and embrace what is true for me. The superhero within me was unleashed, and I would not be where I am today had you not struck that match and shined a light where I needed to see. Thank you also for creating a safe, inclusive, and life-saving space for members of the LGBTQ+ community to be served and supported.

Thank you to my best friend and sister Lisa. You create a safe space for me to be fully accepted and loved in every moment.

Thank you to the victims and survivors that have shared your voices, stories, and courage with me. You give me hope that helps me rise up every single day.

Thank you to my love Michelle, the love of my life. Thank you for choosing to love yourself first and courageously going after what you deserved. Thank you for choosing to love me, my vision, and my purpose, fully and unconditionally. Thank you for sharing your joy, your heartache, your children, your beautiful light, your fire, your koala bear hugs, and your unstoppable force with me. You are a superhero. You are my home. You are my heart. You are a divine goddess that I will always honor and worship. Your heart is safe with me.

To Stella and Oliver. I can't wait to see the superheroes you become, and how both of you superstars will use your personal power for BIG disruption and change. I'll always be here to cheer you on and be your backup when you need it!

Notes/References

Introduction: For it is not the light that is needed, but fire...

1. Smithsonian National Museum of African American History & Culture. A nation's story: "What to the slave is the fourth of July?" Available from: https://nmaahc.si.edu/explore/stories/nations-story-what-slave-fourth-july

2. Columbia Law School. Kimberlé Crenshaw on intersectionality, more than two decades later. (2017, June 8). Available from: www.law.columbia.edu/news/archive/kimberlé-crenshaw-intersectionality-more-two-decades-later

Chapter 1: You are enough

1. R. F. Baumeister and M. R. Leary, "The need to belong: Desire for interpersonal attachments as a fundamental human motivation" in *Psychological Bulletin*, 117 (3), 497–529 (1995). Available from: https://doi.org/10.1037/0033-2909.117.3.497

2. A. Angehrn, A. J. Fletcher, and R. N. Carleton, "'Suck it up, buttercup': Understanding and overcoming gender disparities in policing" in *Int J Environ Res Public Health*, 18 (14), 7627 (2021, July 18). doi: 10.3390/ijerph18147627. PMID: 34300078; PMCID: PMC8304614. Available from: www.ncbi.nlm.nih.gov/pmc/articles/PMC8304614/#:~:text=Women%20police%20officers%20report%20experiencing,their%20men%20colleagues%20%5B20%5D

3. *Avengers: End Game* movie (2019).

Chapter 2: Disrupt the limiting voices and thoughts

1. J. Guttman, "The relationship with yourself" in *Psychology Today*, (2019, June 27). Available from: www.psychologytoday.com/us/blog/sustainable-life-satisfaction/201906/the-relationship-yourself

2. R. Leadem, "12 leaders, entrepreneurs and celebrities who have struggled with imposter syndrome" in *Entrepreneur*, (2017, November 8). Available from: www.entrepreneur.com/leadership/12-leaders-entrepreneurs-and-celebrities-who-have/304273

3. R. Leadem, "These artists, authors and leaders battled self-doubt before they made history" in *Entrepreneur*, (2017, November 9). Available from: www.entrepreneur.com/leadership/these-artists-authors-and-leaders-battled-self-doubt/304340

4. L. Geall, "12 successful women on imposter syndrome and self-doubt" in *Stylist*, (2020). Available from: www.stylist.co.uk/entertainment/celebrity/imposter-syndrome-quotes-elebrities/307473

5. C. L. Exley and J. B. Kessler, "The gender gap in self-promotion" in *National Bureau of Economic Research*, (2019). Available from: www.nber.org/papers/w26345

6. L. Twist. *Living a Committed Life: Finding Freedom and Fulfillment in a Purpose Larger than Yourself.* Bernet-Koehler Publishers, Inc. (2023).

7. N. Morgan, "Yes, optimism, imagery, and self-talk work" in *Psychology Today*, (2022, July 29). Available from: www.psychologytoday.com/us/blog/communications-matter/202207/yes-optimism-imagery-and-self-talk-work

Chapter 3: Be fully and authentically *you* in every moment

1. J. Gaines, "The philosophy of Ikigai: 3 examples about finding purpose" in *Positive Psychology*, (2020, November 17). Available from: https://positivepsychology.com/ikigai

2. K. Miller, "How to increase self-awareness: 16 activities & tools" in *Positive Psychology*, (2020, March 13). Available from: https://positivepsychology.com/building-self-awareness-activities

3. "Top evidence-based benefits of journaling for mental health" in *Reflection. App*, (2022, December 27). Available from: www.reflection.app/blog/benefits-of-journaling

4. T. Smyth, PhD, LMFT/LPCC, "Are women pressured into unhealthy" in Connolly Counseling Centre. Available from: www.counsellor.ie/are-women-pressured-into-unhealthy-people-pleasing

Chapter 5: Use your most powerful tool: Your voice

1. C. Durand, "Duchess Meghan Markle reflects on George Floyd's death in graduation speech for her high school" in *Oprah Daily*, (2020, June 4). Available from: www.oprahdaily.com/entertainment/a32644003/meghan-markle-george-floyd-graduation-speech

2. S. Wolpert, "UCLA neuroscientist's book explains why social connection is as important as food and shelter" in *UCLA Newsroom*, (2013, October 13). Available from: https://newsroom.ucla.edu/releases/we-are-hard-wired-to-be-social-248746

Chapter 6: Lay down your safety

1. E. Field, A. Krivkovick, S. Kugele, N. Robinson, and L. Yee, "Women in the workplace 2023" in *McKinsey & Company*, (2023, October 5). Available from: www.mckinsey.com/featured-insights/diversity-and-inclusion/women-in-the-workplace

2. Sunu P. Chandy, "In support of Rosette Pambakian: 3 ways forced arbitration stacks the deck against sexual harassment survivors" in *National Women's Law Center Blog Post*, (2020, July 7). Available from: https://nwlc.org/in-support-of-rosette-pambakian-3-ways-forced-arbitration-stacks-the-deck-against-sexual-harassment-survivors

3. Alexander J. S. Colvin, "The growing use of mandatory arbitration: Access to the courts is now barred for more than 60 million American workers" in *Economic Policy Institute Report*, (2018, April 6). Available from: www.epi.org/publication/the-growing-use-of-mandatory-arbitration-access-to-the-courts-is-now-barred-for-more-than-60-million-american-workers

4. Kate Hamaji et al., "Unchecked corporate power: Forced arbitration, the enforcement crisis, and how workers are fighting back" in The Center for Popular Democracy, Economic Policy Institute and the National Employment Law Project, (2019, May

144 Match-Striking for Beginners

20). Available from: www.populardemocracy.org/sites/default/
files/Unchecked-Corporate-Power-web.pdf

5. R. Parks. *Rosa Parks: My Story* (1992).

Chapter 8: Collective activation: Move forward with boldness and disruption

1. Tarana Burke, "Tarana Burke: What 'Me Too' Made Possible" in *Time*, (2022, October 12). https://time.com/6221110/tarana-burke-me-too-anniversary

Resources

988 Suicide & Crisis Lifeline (24 hrs)

Call or Text* 988
Free and confidential support for people in distress.
Chat services are also available.
https://988lifeline.org/chat

The Trevor Project Hotline (24 hrs)

Call (866) 488-7386 or Text* START to 678678
Free and confidential support service offering crisis support
to LGBTQ+ young people. The Trevor Project also has a
resource center for young people.
Chat services are also available.
www.thetrevorproject.org

AVP (Anti-Violence Project) (24 hrs)

Call or text (212) 714-1141
Free and confidential crisis intervention hotline offering
support to LGBTQ+ and HIV-affected survivors of any type of
violence, as well as to those who love and support survivors,
including those who have lost a loved one to violence.
The largest anti-LGBTQ violence organization in the U.S.
and coordinates the National Coalition of Anti-Violence
Programs. AVP also provides a range of services including
free legal services.
https://avp.org

Lesbian, Gay, Bisexual, and Transgender (LGBT) National Hotline (24 hrs)

Call (888) 843-4564
Free and confidential LGBTQ+ peer support, information, and local resources.
Chat services are also available.
www.lgbthotline.org

Trans Lifeline Hotline (24 hrs)

Call (877) 565-8860
Free and confidential peer support phone service run by trans people for trans and questioning peers.
https://translifeline.org/hotline

National Sexual Assault Hotline (24 hrs)

Call (800) 656-HOPE (4673)
Free and confidential support for victims/survivors of sexual harassment and sexual violence.
Chat services are also available.
www.rainn.org/resources

National Domestic Violence Hotline (24 hrs)

Call (800) 799-SAFE (7233) or Text* START to 88788
Free and confidential support for victims/survivors of domestic violence.
Chat services are also available.
www.thehotline.org

1in6 Hotline (24 hrs)

Call (800) 656-4673
Free and confidential support service helpline for male victim/survivors of sexual abuse and assault.
Chat services are also available.
https://1in6.org

StrongHearts Native Helpline (24 hrs)

Call or Text* to (844) 7NATIVE (762-8483)
Free and confidential support service for Native American
victims/survivors of domestic and sexual violence.
https://strongheartshelpline.org

Love is Respect (24 hrs)

Call (866) 331-9474 Text* LOVEIS to 22522
Free and confidential support service helpline for dating
abuse.
Chat services are also available.
https://loveisrespect.org

National Human Trafficking Hotline (24 hrs)

Call (888) 373-7888 or Text* 233733
Free and confidential help and support services for you or
someone you know who is a victim of human trafficking. For
general inquiries and information on human trafficking,
including sexual exploitation of children, visit Polaris.org
and Thorn.org.
Chat services are also available.
https://humantraffickinghotline.org/en

NO MORE Global Resource Directory

A comprehensive, global directory of domestic and sexual
violence helplines and services serving international
locations. This global directory also includes services for
communities that are not DV/SA specific. NO MORE is a
global initiative working to amplify and grow the movement
to stop and prevent domestic violence and sexual assault, in
homes, schools, workplaces, and communities around the
world.
https://nomoredirectory.org

National Coalition Against Domestic Violence (NCADV) Resource List

A comprehensive list of resources in the U.S. provided by the NCADV covering a wide variety of needs, including various organizations serving children, teens, people with disabilities, women of color, Latina/Latino, immigrant, Indigenous women, Asian/Pacific Islander, African American, LGBTQ+, abuse in later life, men, and those needing legal resources. https://ncadv.sitewrench.com/resources

Survivor's Sanctuary provided by me too. Movement

A healing support service that includes 36 different self-guided digital lessons between 5 to 25 minutes in length created by Black, Indigenous, and Brown practitioners that explore creating affirmation practices, breathing exercises, and compassionate self-touch. Find more outstanding survivor and community-based action resources at me too. Movement online at **metoomvmt.org** https://sanctuary.metoomvmt.org

Human Rights Campaign (HRC)

Resources and tools for equality and inclusion. The HRC strives to end discrimination against LGBTQ+ people and realize a world that achieves fundamental fairness and equality for all. www.hrc.org/resources

National Women's Law Center

Legal and policy resources. The National Women's Law Center fights for gender justice and advocates for women's rights and LGBTQ+ rights through litigation, policy, and culture change initiatives. https://nwlc.org

Raliance

Raliance advises organizations of all sizes on how to prevent and address sexual harassment, misconduct, and abuse. They provide services that help organizations to change their culture for the better with expert consulting such as organizational assessment, policy review, customized training, internal auditing, and crisis communications guidance. www.raliance.org

The Purple Method

The Purple Method is dedicated to addressing and preventing sexual misconduct. Founded and led by trained experts and legal professionals who are deeply aware of the negative effects sexual harassment can have on psychological well-being and organizational health. The team creates custom anti-harassment solutions custom-tailored to your unique company mission that actually work, designed by experts who know firsthand. www.thepurplemethod.com

Callisto

Ninety per cent of campus sexual assaults are committed by serial perpetrators. Callisto has created an innovative encrypted system—Callisto Vault—that enables survivors to document an assault or match with others harmed by the same perpetrator, whether or not they report or disclose publicly. Matched survivors then receive free and confidential legal options counseling. Not only does this empower survivors but, by facilitating collective action, it increases the likelihood that perpetrators will be held accountable. There is free access for anyone with an.edu email on college campuses. www.projectcallisto.org

The National Network to End Domestic Violence (NNEDV)

NNEDV has a comprehensive online policy center and resource library that includes essential toolkits. NNEDV is a social change organization dedicated to creating a social, political, and economic environment in which violence against women no longer exists.
https://nnedv.org

A Call to Men

A Call to Men works to transform society by promoting healthy, respectful manhood and offering training and educational resources for companies, government agencies, schools, and community groups.
www.acalltomen.org

Ujima

Ujima is The National Center on Violence Against Women in the Black Community and serves as a culturally specific services issue resource center to provide support to and be a voice for the Black community in response to domestic, sexual and community violence.
https://ujimacommunity.org

The Ladies of Hope Ministries (LOHM)

The LOHM provides support services for women and girls who are impacted by the criminal legal system with a mission to empower women and girls to create sustainable lives post-incarceration.
https://thelohm.org

Esperanza United

Resources and help for Latin@ communities impacted by gender-based violence. Founded and led by Latinas,

Esperanza United works with the community, other service providers, and systems to ensure Latinas, their families, and their communities receive culturally relevant advocacy and quality, appropriate, and effective resources.
https://esperanzaunited.org/en

Disability Rights Education and Defense Fund (DREDF)

Legal and policy resources. DREDF is a national civil rights law and policy center directed by individuals with disabilities and parents who have children with disabilities. Their mission is to advance the civil and human rights of people with disabilities through legal advocacy, training, education and public policy, and legislative development.
https://dredf.org

Center for Democracy and Technology (CDT)

The CDT fights to advance civil rights and civil liberties in the digital age with a presence in the U.S. and Europe. The CDT works to promote democratic values by shaping technology policy and architecture, with a focus on the rights of the individual.
https://cdt.org

About the author

Tracey Breeden is a thought leader and Queer activist, life coach, advisor, speaker, and an executive leader, with over two decades as a safety and inclusion expert working in public safety and leading efforts globally in the tech industry. Known as a fearless people leader that fought for and created safe, inclusive, and empowering spaces for both consumers and employees.

Tracey has a vision of building authentic, equitable, and respectful communities, free from harm. She is relentlessly committed to the expansion of that vision, empowering and igniting people to be better, more powerful versions of themselves, unleashing their inner superhero through self-development and activating collective power from the margin—all toward creating a better world.

A former law enforcement officer and medal of valor recipient, Tracey was Uber's first Head of Women's Safety and Gender-Based Violence creating Uber's first global team dedicated to the safety of women and other vulnerable populations. She was the Vice President, Head of Safety and Social Advocacy at Match Group, the parent company of dating apps like Tinder, Hinge, and OkCupid. While there she was named in the top 50 LGBTQ women and non-binary innovators in business and tech, before creating her own coaching and advisory practice.

Tracey has influenced international dialogue on the safety of women and marginalized groups with companies, government officials, and she has been cited by leading news outlets and publications, including the Associated Press,

Reuters, CNN, *The Washington Post, USA Today,* CBS This Morning, Fox Business and TechCrunch.

She is most grateful for the opportunities to share her unique journey, individually and collectively, with others. It's so much more than just creating safe spaces. Through coaching and speaking, she is instrumental in supporting, elevating, and empowering people first, prioritizing the historically marginalized. Tracey doesn't stop at inspiration. She gives you the tools and wisdom she gained through her lived experience and others to accelerate self-development and successfully execute on both your personal and professional desires, while weaving mission into your daily experiences and even your day job!

You can learn more about Tracey and contact her directly for speaking engagements, one-to-one life coaching, and advisory services through her website at traceybreeden.com.

Index

A quick word from Practical Inspiration Publishing...

We hope you found this book both practical and inspiring – that's what we aim for with every book we publish.

We publish titles on topics ranging from leadership, entrepreneurship, HR and marketing to self-development and wellbeing.

Find details of all our books at: www.practicalinspiration.com

 Did you know...

We can offer discounts on bulk sales of all our titles – ideal if you want to use them for training purposes, corporate giveaways or simply because you feel these ideas deserve to be shared with your network.

We can even produce bespoke versions of our books, for example with your organization's logo and/or a tailored foreword.

To discuss further, contact us on info@practicalinspiration.com.

 Got an idea for a business book?

We may be able to help. Find out more about publishing in partnership with us at: bit.ly/PIpublishing.

Follow us on social media...

 @PIPTalking

@pip_talking

@practicalinspiration

@piptalking

Practical Inspiration Publishing

Milton Keynes UK
Ingram Content Group UK Ltd.
UKHW021811030624
443664UK00010B/38

9 781788 606103